THE WORLD'S ECONOMIC CRISIS

THE
HALLEY STEWART TRUST

FOUNDED 15TH DECEMBER 1924
FOR RESEARCH TOWARDS THE CHRISTIAN IDEAL IN ALL
SOCIAL LIFE.

The objects of the Trust are *in general:*

To advance religion; to advance education; to relieve poverty; to promote other Charitable purposes beneficial to the community, and *in particular:*

1. To assist in the discovery of the best means by which "the mind of Christ" may be applied to extending the Kingdom of God by the prevention and removal of human misery;

2. To assist in the study of our Lord's life and teaching in their explicit and implicit application to the social relationships of man;

3. To express the mind of Christ in the realization of the Kingdom of God upon earth and in a national and a world-wide brotherhood;

For example:

For every Individual, by furthering such favourable opportunities of education, service, and leisure as shall enable him or her most perfectly to develop the body, mind and spirit:

In all Social Life, whether domestic, industrial, or national, by securing a just environment, and

In International Relationships, by fostering good will between all races, tribes, peoples, and nations so as to secure the fulfilment of the hope of "peace on earth";

4. To provide fees for a Lecture or Lectures annually and prizes for essays or other written compositions, and to pay for their publication and distribution;

5. To provide, maintain, and assist Lectures and Research work in Social, Economic, Psychological, Medical, Surgical, or Educational subjects;

6. To make grants to Libraries;

7. To assist publications exclusively connected with the objects of the Trust (not being newspapers or exclusively denominational);

8. To make grants to and co-operate with Societies, Organizations, and Persons engaged in the furtherance of Charitable objects similar to the objects of the Trust;

9. To use the foregoing and any such other methods, whether of a like nature or not, as are lawful and reasonable and appropriate for the furtherance of the objects of the Trust.

The income of the Trust may not be used for dogmatic theological or ecclesiastical purposes other than the cult of the Science of God as manifest in man in the Son of Man in the person and teaching of Our Lord, "The Word of God," Who "liveth and abideth forever."

1926
Science and Human Progress
By SIR OLIVER LODGE

"A valuable work, courageous, comprehensive, and simply expressed."—*Quarterly Review*

Third Impression

1927
Christ and Society
By BISHOP GORE, D.D., LL.D.

"With the zeal of a prophet Dr. Gore recalls his fellow-disciples to the first principles of Christian faith and fellowship."—*Times Literary Supplement*

Second Impression

1928
The Ordeal of this Generation
By GILBERT MURRAY, LL.D., D.LITT.

"The reader will be dull indeed who does not appreciate the beautiful coherence of argument."

Times Literary Supplement
Third Impression

1929
Equality
By R. H. TAWNEY, D.LITT.

"The dignified beauty of its style, the wide range of its knowledge, the serried vigour of its argument, make it a contribution of high importance to social theory."—H. J. Laski in the *Week-end Review*

Revised Cheaper Second Edition

1930
Health and Social Evolution
By SIR GEORGE NEWMAN, K.C.B., M.D.,
F.R.C.P., LL.D.

"Bears on every page the stamp of expert knowledge, generous humanism, and the broadest literary culture."

British Weekly

THE
WORLD'S ECONOMIC CRISIS

AND THE WAY OF ESCAPE

by

Sir Arthur Salter, K.C.B.
Sir Josiah Stamp, K.B.E.
J. Maynard Keynes, M.A.
Sir Basil Blackett, K.C.B.
Henry Clay, M.A., D.Sc.
Sir W. H. Beveridge, K.C.B.

NEW YORK
THE CENTURY CO.

First Printing

CONTENTS

I

SIR ARTHUR SALTER

FROM WHO'S WHO (1932)

SALTER, SIR JAMES ARTHUR, K.C.B., *cr.* 1922; C.B. 1918; Director Economic and Finance Section League of Nations, June 1919, Jan. 1920, and 1922–30; General Secretary Reparation Commission, 1920–22; *b.* Oxford, 15 March, 1881; *s.* of James E. Salter, Oxford; unmarried. *Educ.:* Oxford High School; Brasenose College, Oxford, First Class Classical Moderations, 1901; First Class Literæ Humaniores; Senior Hulme Scholarship, 1903. Higher Division Clerk Transport Department, Admiralty, 1904; Assistant Secretary National Health Insurance Commission, England, 1913; Assistant Director of Transports, Admiralty, 1915; Director of Ship Requisitioning, 1917; Secretary of Allied Maritime Transport Council and Chairman of Allied Maritime Transport Executive, 1918; Special Shipping Mission to America, May 1918; Secretary, British Department, Supreme Economic Council, 1919; Officier de la Couronne Belgique, 1919; Commandeur de la Legion d'Honneur, 1920; Commendatore Order of the Crown of Italy, 1922. *Publication:* Allied Shipping Control: An Experiment in International Administration, 1921.

I

SIR ARTHUR SALTER

THE title of these lectures is *The World's Economic Crisis and the Way of Escape*. I must say at once that this is not a promise to show a "way of escape" subscribed to by the six authors. We do our best to make suggestions, but we do not bring any simple panacea—indeed we do not even bring a concerted policy. So far as we have different views of policy we have expressed them and you can judge between us. So far as we do express the same views it will be because of a real identity of opinion and not the result of any concerted agreement or compromise arranged between us.

I wish to congratulate the Halley Stewart Trustees upon the choice of my co-authors for this book, and for one reason in particular. They are not only economists, but they all have practical and direct experience in public affairs, in business or in finance. I am not myself in the strict sense an economist. But for over a quarter of a century I have been engaged as a public official in work which has constantly needed both the guidance of economic doctrine and the practical co-operation of business men.

I have always been impressed with the fact that there is too often a regrettable separation between Doctrine and Practice. And a solution to our present difficulties will, I believe, only come from a fruitful union between the two.

There have been faults on both sides. Too often the economist withdraws to a closed world of theory, like an anchorite to his cell, sometimes inclined even to think that his professional integrity is violated by any close contact with practical affairs; or, turning to the other extreme, he has become merely a narrative and descriptive historian, losing any guiding thread of principle in the maze of his facts. On the other hand, the practical man too often takes a short and a narrow view, is inclined to snatch a sectional and a momentary advantage—and to persuade his Government to help him in that disastrous process. The five experts who follow me are exempt from either charge.

Though we have no concerted policy, we have arranged a rough division of our subject. I myself deal with the general world position and make suggestions for a world policy; Sir Josiah Stamp deals with the special difficulties and problems of Great Britain; then Mr. Maynard Keynes discusses the immediate tasks ahead; Sir Basil Blackett urges the need of deliberate planning ahead and of a far-sighted programme of work and policy; next, Mr. Henry Clay discusses unemployment; and Sir William Beveridge in the last lecture will summarize what we have said, finding harmony between our views where it exists, and making his own comments where it does not.

My task, then, is to speak of the general world situation. My first comment is this. It is important that we should remember that if the world has now had two and a half years of a very severe depression, it had, before that depression began, made an extraordinarily rapid recovery from the devastation of the war. When at Paris, in 1919, we looked at a world shattered in four years of destructive war—at the shortages on every hand, the dislocation and the disorganization—none of us ventured to hope that early recovery would be possible. Many indeed thought that the whole economic system was collapsing and that we should fall into complete chaos, or at least to a substantially lower level of civilization before we took the upward turn again. In fact, however, recovery was extremely rapid, although, as we now see, it was based to some extent on unsound foundations and subject to certain latent weaknesses which have since become evident. Within seven years of the conclusion of the war the world as a whole was substantially better off than it had been before the war. Production had increased more rapidly than population. The average standard of living was higher. Belligerent Europe had fallen a little behind, but it made up in the next few years, and in 1929, only about ten years after the conclusion of hostilities, not only the world as a whole, but even Europe, had a higher average standard of living than in 1913. That was an amazing achievement. Man proved a much more adaptable creature than anyone in 1919 would have thought possible.

What was done then we can do again; and we can do it better; we can build on more secure foundations. It is true that the second effort we have now to make is in some respects more painful than the first. In 1919 we felt that the waste around us was caused by a temporary and a past disaster. Now that we have to face the trouble that has developed in ten years of peace and growing prosperity, we may naturally feel that the causes are more obscure and more difficult to deal with. We have now to gird ourselves to the second and more painful effort.

Throughout these lectures we must distinguish three problems, though they interact. First there is the special position of this country, with which Sir Josiah Stamp deals. Our difficulties have been aggravated and altered by the world depression, but to a large extent they existed before it and are due to other causes. In the early part of 1929, when the world as a whole enjoyed great prosperity, we had great unemployment and had for almost four years been steadily losing our relative position in world trade. We must not, therefore, assume that when the world depression has passed our own difficulties will be over too. We have next to consider the world economic depression that began in the autumn of 1929, to examine its causes and characteristics, and follow its course for one and three-quarter years; and then thirdly we must look at the world financial crisis that began in June 1931 and see how it has since affected the economic depression and the general world situation.

The first thing I wish to remark is that this is obviously in the fullest sense a world depression. Its causes, certainly, did not originate in any one country, or, indeed, in any one continent. Its effects extend over the whole of the habitable world. Here and there folly or misfortune may aggravate the position, but one after another all countries have been brought within the extending circle of disaster. The depression is world-wide in its origins and the range of its effects. And it seems to me perfectly clear, too, that any remedies that can effectively deal with the situation must have a world character as well. No national policy alone can suffice. Concerted policy alone will be adequate for the task.

Not only is this depression world-wide; it is very complicated in causes and character. There is a very natural human disposition, when a man feels pain anywhere, to hope there is some single specific cause and some single specific remedy, but I am afraid the malady from which the world is now suffering is not of a simple character; and no single specific panacea will be sufficient.

There was once an ingenious theory that depression was due to sun-spots, which were supposed to cause bad harvests, and so to start a process of impoverishment. We have heard nothing of that theory this time, because the harvests have obviously been not bad but abundant. But some people have talked as if the simple explanation, once afforded by sun-spots, was now afforded by silver. They are certainly wrong. I will not say that silver counts for nothing at all in this depression, but my own very strong view is that it occupies a very small place indeed in it. Others ascribe as the cause of the depression one of several factors, each of which is indeed important, but none of which occupies a sole or dominant position. Some say, for example, that it is due to a scarcity or misuse of gold; others that the whole trouble arises out of reparation and war debts; others from the world's commercial policies and tariffs. Well, I believe all those three factors have been very substantial contributory factors. But certainly I do not believe that any one of them is the sole, or indeed a very predominant, factor. I think it is the combination of them with certain other factors which I shall mention a little later on which caused the trouble.

What then is this world depression? It clearly is not due to any inadequacy of Nature's resources.

It clearly is not due to any inadequacy of man's industrial skill or scientific knowledge. Nor is it due to any insufficiency of human demand for things which Nature and Science can provide us with. Human demand, I do not say effective economic demand but human demand, is illimitable and will be until the last Hottentot lives like a millionaire.

But, of course, human demand is a different thing from effective purchasing power, effective demand. In my view the most general description of the character of this depression is that somehow or other the ability to produce, which the world has in abundance, has been unable to translate itself (as normally it should, and in happier times it did) into an ability to purchase to an equal extent. Somehow or other, in that long, intricate chain which connects together all the processes of production—making, selling, consuming—something has broken or become blocked or defective.

This is not the first time we have had a difficulty of that kind; though it is the first time that it has been upon the present scale. Our best approach to our subject is therefore to consider what an ordinary depression in a trade cycle is, and then what are the aggravating factors which have so intensified and enlarged the scale of this particular depression that it has become something different, not only in degree but in kind.

I shall not try to give a scientific description of

the trade cycle. With sufficient precision for the present argument I may describe it as follows. Under stable conditions and with advancing prosperity each manufacturer in an industry, planning separately on what scale he will produce, has to estimate what will be the future demand for his type of article and what proportion of the market he will be able to capture. With a natural human optimism he tends to overestimate both. Output outruns demand. Supplies are thrown on the market at unprofitable prices. Expenditure on new plant is stopped. The purchasing power of all concerned is reduced and the depression spreads until the reduced prices again stimulate demand.

What are aggravating factors which account for the peculiar intensity of this depression?

I will first mention four which are independent of the war or war policy, and would in any case have caused trouble on a bigger scale than we used to know in the nineteenth century.

In the first place the large scale of the organization of modern businesses sometimes makes them less flexible to sudden changes in demand and in price. When most articles were produced by innumerable individual manufacturers, output almost necessarily fell very quickly when prices ceased to be profitable because a firm could not afford to go on. The consequence does not always follow so quickly where a large part of the output comes from powerful firms who may continue production for some time after it has ceased to be profitable, hoping for a revival of the market. In addition, there is now a greater rigidity of price levels and wage levels with consequences that are familiar to us all.

Next, demand tends to be more capricious. This is very largely because the world is now more prosperous; there is a very much bigger margin of purchasing power after the bare necessities of life have been paid for. A larger proportion of what the world buys is in the nature of articles of additional comfort or of luxury. It is natural that the demand for these things should be more capricious or changeable, varying with taste and fashion, and therefore more difficult to calculate than the great basic necessities of food, housing and clothing. Consequently the people who are planning production all over the world have a more difficult problem to face.

In the third place, we are now between two different systems, each of which will work, but which in combination I will not say are impossible, but are difficult. On the one hand there is the old competitive automatic adjustment of changing prices, to which we were accustomed before the war, the changing price adjusting supply to demand; this is now less effective because in a hundred ways competition is either being stopped or impeded or changing its form.

On the other hand, there is, as in Russia, the

alternative system of deliberate planning. This does not give the stimulus to production or the flexible and automatic adjustments which changing prices do at their best, but it does introduce an alternative method of adjusting supply to demand.

At the present time we have enough interference with free competition, partly by the way in which industry is organized and partly through various forms of governmental control and interference, to prevent the automatic system working effectively; while organization is still not on a sufficient scale for the alternative method of deliberate planning. To some extent we have lost the advantages of the one system while not getting the advantages of the other.

I do not mean to conclude from this that we should or can go back to the freely working competitive system of the nineteenth century. That is, I think, for many reasons impracticable. Nor do I mean that we should turn to another system which requires the abolition of free political institutions, and the destruction of private liberty and initiative. I still believe that it is possible to combine real initiative, real political freedom, with an element of deliberate planning.

Fourthly, there is one other factor in this depression which is independent of the war, the mechanization of grain production. I believe that if there had never been a general economic depression at all, and never an industrial depression, and never a war, we should still have had at about this period an agricultural depression. The mechanization which we know so much better in the industrial field has now been applied to agriculture too. But there are great differences in the consequences of mechanization in agriculture and in industry. Each has the same result of immensely increasing the yield per human unit. But in the one case it is possible to increase the demand correspondingly. The desire for industrial products is practically illimitable. The man who walks gets a bicycle, and the man who rides a bicycle takes to a motor-car, and after all this he takes the radio and the gramophone, and so on, *ad infinitum*. The human stomach, however, is not so elastic. Generally speaking, a man does not eat more in bulk, although he may eat more in money when he becomes richer. On the whole, indeed, in advanced countries a man eats a little less grain as he becomes better off. It is instructive to see that in America, decade after decade, as the country became more prosperous the average consumption of wheat flour per head has gone down.

It follows that the demand for wheat and grain tends to increase no more rapidly than population, whereas mechanization means that output increases very much more rapidly than population. In the second place, an industrial worker, though not very easily transferable, is much more transferable than a peasant on the soil. It is much more difficult when there is an excess in the production of grain to adjust that by transference from one form of work to another.

Then again in one respect the demand for grain has been reduced. A quarter of a century ago a very large proportion indeed of the transport power of the world was grain fed. Now the oat-consuming horse has been replaced by the petrol engine.

For those reasons, if there had never been any war at all, and if there had been no industrial depression, we should, I think, have had an agricultural depression in the great grain-producing countries at about this time in the world's history. As it happened, the agricultural depression has, largely by a coincidence, supervened on a general depression.

So much for the reasons that are independent of the war. I now come to a number which clearly arise out of the war period. In the first place there are reparation and war debts. It is important to take the true measure of this obstacle to economic recovery. Reparation is paid by a few countries, Germany, Austria, Hungary and Bulgaria, to a considerable number of others. Most of the latter countries pass on what they receive as reparation to other countries to which they owe war debts. The process ultimately means, if we take reparation and war debts together, that of about £80 million paid in a year, three-quarters has been finding its way to America and the rest to France. That is a rough statement but sufficient for my general argument to-night. This sum represents something which has to be paid from one part of the world to another. It must either be paid by the passage of extra goods or it may be paid for a time by loan operations; but there it is, weighing down on the system of international exchange. Between countries to whom money is owed, and those which owe, there is in a normal year a difference of about £400 million sterling. That is to say, the situation before the crisis was: to maintain the national balance of payments, about £400 million sterling of new lending per annum was needed from creditor countries. In that £400 million, reparation and war debt accounted for £80 million, that is about one-fifth. In reality, however, they were more important than this proportion suggests for two reasons. First of all reparation is a deadweight charge. It represents expenditure or waste in a past war. It has no counterpart in an earning industrial asset. Let me explain that. A large part of the £400 million represented loans used for constructive purposes, such as building railways in the Argentine. When a loan is so used the current earnings of the enterprise so financed normally more than pay the annual charges of the loan itself. That involves no strain at all comparable to what is caused by reparation, which is represented by no earning asset. In the second place, reparation is inevitably involved with political conditions and political dangers, of which the occupation of the Ruhr in 1923 is one example. It therefore makes the basic political condition of the world unstable. The investor alternates between undue optimism and undue pessimism, and there is not that steady confidence upon which the economic structure of the world is best based.

This is the first of the special factors which have weighed on the life of the world and increased this depression. Had it been only one, the world could have carried it. Had the countries to whom, in the last resort, reparation is paid, America and France, been prepared to take what is due to them in the form of additional imports and to adjust their policy towards that end, reparation and war debts could have been paid, on a reasonable scale, without disastrous dislocations. Unhappily that has not been the case.

Next, we have the whole question of gold and gold prices. I cannot go into this problem to-night. I will only make this remark as to how it affects the depression. When a country like America or France is owed money in respect of war debts, other past loans, or reparation, or exports, it can only be paid by taking goods as imports, or out of the proceeds of new loans, or by taking gold. Imports have, however, been blocked by tariffs; lending has practically stopped because of the loss of confidence. Gold has therefore flowed to these two countries from those which owed them money. This gold was, however, not wanted as the basis of currency, and has not, in fact, been used as a basis of as large a volume of money and credit as in the countries from which it came. This is what is meant by saying that there is a "maldistribution" of gold and that it has been "sterilized." The consequence has been that the effective money in the world has been reduced. There is enough gold in the world to support a higher level of prices than the present one if it were properly distributed. Scarcity of gold was not, I think, the initiating cause of the fall of prices; but, rendered less effective by maldistribution, gold has tended to consolidate a fall due to other causes instead of exercising a corrective function. (A VOICE: Why don't you call it cornering?)

I do not call it that because I do not think the drain on gold has been due to deliberate policy. It has reflected the net result of a lot of other operations. When people put up a high tariff in America they do not do it in order to get gold, but to keep other people's goods out. That is the result but not the purpose. That is why I do not call it a cornering of gold.

Prices having fallen and remained low, there has been a heavy weight upon the whole enterprise and initiative of the world, because the obligations of the active part of the world to the inactive have been proportionately increased.

Take, for example, the agricultural producing countries. The value of their products has fallen by about fifty per cent. That means that a producer who has contracted a debt in terms of gold finds that his burden is doubled. The Argentine, for example, has to supply twice as much food and raw materials to pay interest on debentures as it had to pay before the fall in prices. As the indebtedness of one part of the world to the other was already exceptionally high, this enormous increase has made it intolerable.

The next cause I will mention is the reckless borrowing, particularly by Governments and public authorities, in the years just before the depression. This is rarely cited amongst the principal causes of the depression. But I believe myself that it is a very big factor indeed. A very large proportion of the money lent abroad from one country to another, to Governments and public authorities in the four years preceding the economic depression, was wasted. When it was wasted the resulting obligation assumed the same character as reparation; that is to say, it became a deadweight obligation which cannot be met by the earnings of an economic asset.

I say "reckless borrowing"; but perhaps I should say reckless lending, because a large part of the responsibility must fall on the powerful issuing houses

which lent money to small countries in eastern
Europe or South America. A very great deal of
money was lent and obligations contracted, and the
money used or misused without leaving anything
behind in the form of productive earning assets.

Lastly, as a cause immediately precipitating the
depression, there was the speculative boom in
America and the crash that followed it in the autumn of 1929.

When the depression had continued for nearly
two years it was intensified by the financial crisis
of June 1931. For years past the whole economic
system had come to depend upon continuous new
lending by creditor countries. But as the depression
continued, the investor naturally became anxious as
to the solvency of the debtors; he became reluctant
to invest or lend in any way which did not enable
him to get his money back quickly. In 1930, therefore, debtors became more and more dependent
upon advances recallable at short notice. This was a
very precarious foundation for the world's economy,
for it was liable to collapse at the first serious shock
to confidence.

Various political incidents gave this shock in the
early part of 1931. There was a run on the short-
term advances. It was soon evident that they could
not be repaid. This constituted the financial crisis.
And it has in practically every respect deepened the
depression.

For when a country owes more than is due to it and cannot borrow, it can only meet its obligations by parting with its gold, or by exporting more than it imports. We have therefore seen first a new drain on gold from debtor countries which has increased the maldistribution and then driven most countries off the gold standard. Meantime the frantic efforts of the same countries to redress their balance of trade by cutting off imports have reduced world trade, and their attempts to increase their exports at any cost have again driven down world prices.

In this last year the situation has got out of control. The adjustments required are not being made by deliberate policy, but by the clash of brute facts and forces. Unless the regulative wisdom of the world can resume control we are rapidly approaching the point at which there will be hardly any world trade at all, except in those few articles which can neither be dispensed with nor made at home.

I now come to remedies.

First, reparation and war debt, already suspended, must obviously be suspended for a longer period. They must also be greatly reduced. And it is of great importance that it should be known soon what the ultimate payments will be, and that they will be moderate enough to be obviously well within the capacity of the debtor countries.

Next, we need reform in monetary policy. I should like to see gold prices brought back to the level at which they stood in 1929 before the depression began. And after that I should like to see an approximate stability in the general price level. If the first could be achieved, a new stimulus would be given to enterprise, and the burden of debt, both public and private, would be lightened. If the second were possible, recovery, once attained, would have a much better chance of being permanent.

I believe both are practicable if the world really desires them. Gold prices could be raised if countries with a gold surplus would use their gold to create a bigger volume of credit and money; in other words, if there were a limited inflation in America and France. This would increase imports into these countries—and indeed would be useless if it were prevented from doing so by new tariffs. To facilitate imports is not popular, of course, especially when home industries are depressed. But now that lending has stopped, and debtor countries can no longer send substantial quantities of gold, the balance of trade creditor countries must be changed. This can only be done by an increase of imports or a loss of exports, or both. To the extent to which imports are welcomed, exports will be saved. There are, of course, difficulties, both technical and political, but they are not insuperable; and America appears to be now contemplating action of this nature.

So, too, when a tolerable level of world prices has

been regained, the level could afterwards be kept reasonably stable, if the world were agreed and determined. Central banks in co-operation could, within certain limits, maintain short-term stability by their customary methods. When a continuing scarcity or excess of gold was found too strong for them the gold content of currencies could be simultaneously and equally changed. If, for example, a gold scarcity of, say, 10 per cent. was likely to force prices down, all countries could simultaneously devalue their currencies by a similar percentage and correct this tendency. Such a devaluation, if simultaneous and adjusted only to prevent a fall in the world level of prices, would be open to none of the ordinary objections to devaluation. It would neither cause exchange fluctuations nor involve injustice to creditors.

One word as to the policy of countries now off the Gold Standard. More than half the world is now in this category. We are among those who have for the time abandoned gold. The policy I would like our country, and others in the same position, to pursue is this. We should make our main objective the substantial maintenance of the internal purchasing value of our national currencies. This objective should, I think, dominate every sphere of policy, including that of tariffs, because internal purchasing value is the only anchor of real value once gold has been left; and if this anchor drags there is no saying how far our currency might depreciate. I do not say that there should be no increase of prices, or the cost of living, at all. Indeed, I think there must be some increase, unless gold prices fall farther. But it ought not to be enough to disturb the main wage and cost of production level. There is some margin, for the cost of living has fallen by 11 per cent. in two years, and it might well go up to some extent without causing a change in the wage and cost levels. If we can successfully maintain the purchasing value of the pound in this way, and to this extent, we should have a currency both useful to ourselves and respected by other countries. Those who have followed us off gold might follow us in this policy. They might look to us as a leader. We could concert our policy together; establish stability of exchange with each other; and limit the fluctuations of our exchange with the gold countries.

This would have great advantages. First, it would mean that if it proves impossible to secure the conditions required to enable the Gold Standard to function reasonably well in future, we should at least have a tolerable alternative. A managed currency, without a metallic basis, is perilous and difficult, but it is not impossible. And certainly the perils will be less if we work out the problems which it involves carefully and in concert with other countries; and do not incur the further risks of attempting it separately, with no basis of a concerted international policy to support it, and without sufficient preparation.

But secondly, to be prepared if necessary to use a concerted managed currency gives a better chance of not being forced to rely upon it. For it would give us—the countries now off gold—a much stronger bargaining position in the very difficult negotiations with the gold countries.

Next, tariff and commercial policies must be reformed. Neither world trade nor a world monetary policy is compatible with nationalistic economic policy.

Next, we need to try to restore foreign lending as soon as possible. This will be difficult. It means the re-establishment of confidence very badly shaken; and I think it will be a long time at the best before the investor will again be prepared to lend abroad on the same scale as before the depression. Special measures of encouragement may be necessary. But they need to be accompanied by precautions to prevent the gross abuses of the past recurring, to ensure that the investor is better safeguarded against his money being wasted on unproductive enterprises. And this is a problem that needs to be taken in hand while the investor is still reluctant.

Lastly, as the indispensable foundation of any tolerable world economic structure, we need assured

SIR ARTHUR SALTER

peace in the world; and for that a strengthening of
the "collective system" of the Covenant of the
League of Nations. Man can never hope for more
than brief and precarious periods of prosperity if
the sword of Damocles hangs always over him.

This is a very brief summary of the kind of
remedies I should like to see the world in concert
take to get out of our present difficulties. We have,
I am afraid, still a rather dreary prospect before us,
certainly for the next few months to come. World
trade is still going down month by month. We are
rapidly approaching the point, as I said, when it
will become as it was, let us say, before the Industrial Revolution, the mere exchange of those products which can be neither dispensed with nor made
at home.

But as we get near this point the world will have
another chance of redressing its policy. World trade
will have demonstrated its value by its disappearance; tariffs will have been equalized by being lev-
elled up—and can perhaps be then more easily
negotiated down. The world must choose between
a policy of national self-sufficiency, partial at the
best, and always impoverishing, and the enrichment
of world trade. Will the gesture of each country to
the others be the gesture of the clenched fist or the
gesture of the open hand? This is the choice that
all the great countries of the world will have to
make again in the months ahead of us. If the world

makes the wiser choice it may advance continuously to higher levels of prosperity; and prosperity and peace may be safely and permanently assured. If it chooses the other, prosperity at the best must be upon a lower level—and it is much more likely to be destroyed by the shattering interruption of war.

The immediate prospect is in some respects a bleak one. But let me remind you, in conclusion, that the problems before us, difficult as they are, are essentially capable of human solution. If either Nature or Science were failing us we might have no alternative but to endure. But our difficulties come only from defects in human organization. And what man has made, man can reform.

We need better organization and regulative wisdom; magnanimity in policy and courage in action. For world problems it is not enough to think nationally, or even imperially, we must think internationally.

II

SIR JOSIAH STAMP

FROM WHO'S WHO (1932)

STAMP, SIR JOSIAH (CHARLES), G.B.E., *cr.* 1924; K.B.E., *cr.* 1920; C.B.E. 1918; Hon. D.Sc. Oxford; Hon. Sc.D. Cambridge; Hon. LL.D. Harvard, Dublin, and Columbia; D.Sc. (Econ.) London; Hon. Member Society Incorporated Accountants and Auditors; F.B.A. 1926; Chairman of the London Midland and Scottish Railway, and President of the Executive; Director of the Bank of England; Member of the Economic Advisory Council; President' Royal Statistical Society, 1930–32; *b.* 21 June, 1880; *e. s.* of Charles Stamp, Yomah, Bexley; *m.* 1903, Olive, *d.* of Alfred Marsh, Grove Park; four *s. Educ.:* London University (Faculty of Economics and Political Science). B.Sc. First Class Hons. 1911; Cobden Prizeman, 1912; D.Sc. 1916; Hutchinson Research Medallist, 1916; Newmarch Lecturer in Statistics, 1919–21, 1923; Member of the Senate, 1924–26, and of the Board of Studies in Economics and other University Committees; at various times Examiner (Economics, Political Science, Statistics, etc.) for Cambridge, London, Edinburg, and Glasgow Universities, and Society of Incorporated Accountants; Guy Medallist of Royal Statistical Society, 1919; Joint Secretary and Editor, 1920–30; Member of International Statistical Institute; Hon. Member American Statistical Association; President British Association (Sec. F), Oxford, 1926; First Beckly Lecturer on Social Service (York Wesleyan Conference, 1926); Sidney Ball Lecturer, Oxford, 1926; Rede Lecturer, Cambridge, 1927; Member of Councils of the Royal Economic and Eugenic Societies, British Academy, etc.; Vice-President, Institute of Industrial Psychology; President Abbey Road Permanent Building Society; President of the Institute of Transport, 1929–30; Vice-Chairman of London School of Economics, Governor of Birkbeck College, of College of Estate Management, of University College, Aberystwyth, of the Leys School, and Chairman of Queenswood School; Chairman Rockefeller Social Science Advisory Committee Pilgrim Trustee; Lieutenant of

[28]

the City of London; Colonel (R. E.) Transport and Railway Corps; General Treasurer of British Association for Advancement of Science; Member, Royal Commission on Income Tax, 1919; Member, Northern Ireland Finance Arbitration Committee, 1923–24; Member, Committee on Taxation and National Debt, 1924; British representative on the Reparation Commission's (Dawes) Committee on German Currency and Finance, 1924, and upon (Young) Experts' Committee, 1929; Member Court of Inquiry, Coal Mining Industry Dispute, 1925; Statutory Commissioner under London University Act, 1926; Chairman of Grain Futures Inquiry, Canada, 1931; entered Civil Service, 1896; Inland Revenue Dept., 1896; Board of Trade (Marine Dept.), 1898; Inland Revenue (Taxes), 1900; transferred to Secretariat, 1914; Assistant Secretary to the Board, 1916; resigned, Mar. 1919; Sec. and Director Nobel Industries, Ltd., 1919–26; Director Imperial Chemical Industries, 1927–28. *Publications:* British Incomes and Property; the Application of Official Statistics to Economic Problems, 1916 (3rd ed. 1922); Wealth and Income of the Chief Powers, 1919; The Fundamental Principles of Taxation in the Light of Modern Developments, 1921 (2nd ed. 1923); Wealth and Taxable Capacity, 1922 (2nd ed. 1923); Joint Report on Double Taxation (League of Nations), 1923; (with C. H. Nelson, Business Statistics and Finance Statements) 1924; Studies in Current Problems in Government and Finance, 1924; Report on Effect of Reparation Payments on Industry (International Chamber of Commerce), 1925; British edition of Rignano's Social Significance of Death Duties, 1925; The Christian Ethic as an Economic Factor, 1926; Articles in Encycl. Brit., 13th and 14th eds.; The National Income, 1924 (with Prof. Bowley), 1926; On Stimulus, 1927; Some Economic Factors in Modern Life, 1928; The Financial Aftermath of War, 1931; Criticism and Other Addresses, 1931; Internationalism, 1931; Papers on Gold and The Price Level, 1931; Taxation during the War, 1932.

II

SIR JOSIAH STAMP

WHEN one elects to discuss a subject like this there is rather an expectation that, after diagnosis, there will follow a series of exact, acceptable and infallible remedies. Unfortunately the present crisis is of such dimensions and such complexity that these hopes have to be disappointed at the outset. A greater service is rendered, I think, by provoking thought amongst one's hearers rather than by attempting to lay down any cut-and-dried solutions. There are two attitudes of mind that always meet anybody who is lecturing on this subject. If one devotes oneself mainly to setting out the causes of the crisis, people impatiently say: "Yes, but what we really want to know is, what is to be done?" If, on the other hand, one devotes one's time to setting out a series of remedies and solutions, they are nearly always unacceptable. People are so impatient of anything unpalatable that their minds are practically inhibited from accepting them outright. There must be an easier path! It is only when inevitability is borne in upon people's minds by a process of elimination that some of the remedies can possibly be accepted with anything like intellectual conviction.

Sir Arthur Salter has dealt in the main with the conditions and causes of the crisis, laying the greatest emphasis on conditions abroad. My part is to deal with a diagnosis of more domestic questions. Mr. Keynes will devote himself to sketching out what he imagines to be the immediate programme in front of us, and later lectures will deal with the more long-distance programme. You must remember that the immediate programme may be very different from the long-distance programme, and may even appear to be receding from it. We have great immediate questions to deal with, and the time has not arrived when we can see exactly where we are going or know whether the immediate programme will fit into the long-distance programme. We may have to go back before we can go forward.

I hope I may be forgiven if I deal in the main with diagnosis, and only generally and perhaps sketchily with either the immediate or long-distance remedies. The part allotted to me is really more difficult, in that it is more sensitive than that taken by Sir Arthur Salter, for it touches you and me—it comes home. No hard-and-fast line can be drawn between what happens abroad and events nearer home. It is impossible to divide the territory so as completely to separate what happens abroad and what are matters of domestic concern. In the first place, there are external questions which, as they change, affect us. Take, for example, the extent to which our export trade is at the present time being encouraged owing to the depreciation of sterling. Obviously the number of countries that go off the Gold Standard affects that particular impetus to our recovery, and that is an outside condition which has an influence upon our economic affairs. So we cannot be indifferent to what happens abroad. In the second place, there are situations here which have become critical only because of outside pressure. We might, for example, be going on quite happily in a particular industry, sustaining a particular standard of life for its workers if there were no competition from abroad, but something may now happen which may make our position in that industry untenable. Take, for example, the pressure of reparation payments, which may enormously affect our export trade in neutral markets. Relief from reparation payments, and from the forced export surplus of Germany or of any country liable for the payment of a heavy external debt, may have important counter-effects upon the ability to maintain a particular wage level because of changes of a monetary character in the wage levels of competing industries abroad, such as a German or Mussolini "cut" in wages.

In the third place, many slightly critical matters may become desperate because of external conditions. There are many questions which are quite manageable as they stand, but which have a potentiality of difficulty if outside pressure acts upon them, if a change in conditions abroad puts pressure upon us. For example, we may have a particular rate of exchange for sterling into foreign currency, dollars or francs, which is conformable to or consistent with a certain balance of trade on physical lines that may just hold the trade situation in equilibrium. Then in a foreign money market some intense domestic pressure may arise. It may be their fear of not being immediately liquid, or there may be other reasons quite unconnected with us, but relating entirely to their own domestic affairs and difficulties which lead to a material and physical call for balances in sterling, and that in turn may lead quite quickly to a "run" of a psychological kind on sterling. It may be possible for a real physical adjustment to affect exchanges, say, by twenty points in one market and for other markets to become scared by that twenty points, and for that scare to carry it to fifty points. Therefore, however stable we may keep our own conditions, however much we may try to reform our own household, whatever steps we may take to get into equilibrium, something may happen abroad which may make our position worse and our task more difficult.

I have to give emphasis to our own conditions, and if in doing so I take only one or two of the chief lines of argument, it must not be supposed that I am oblivious to other aspects of the question. For instance, I shall say very little on the question of rationalization, and of the extent to which by that process we may lower our costs and thereby achieve the same output with less expenditure of human and capital effort. I am going to say very little about that matter, important though it may be in resecuring equilibrium in our export markets. One of the most astonishing things one finds when dealing with the diagnosis of our position, either as it was two years ago when this country was in itself depressed, as distinct from world depression, or as the position is to-day when added to that depression we have our share in the world depression, is the extraordinary divergence between the emphasis laid by foreigners on certain matters and the emphasis laid on other matters by ourselves. It is a difference of approach, and the difference in emphasis is most significant. We start off with the gold price level and other such questions, but the foreigner seems always to come at us from a different angle. He points out the extraordinary decline in our relative and absolute positions as regards exports, and says that there is an urgent necessity for us to reconstruct our national economic structure. This thought of reconstruction instead of restoration is a thought that may come to us when we are compelled to it, but it comes to us late in the argument, whereas it is always first with the foreigner. He sees the unemployment problem—not the present one, but the one that a little while ago seemed to be persistent and chronic, when we had what he would call the "irreducible million" of unemployed—in the light of the development of this country in the latter part of the nineteenth century, and says: "You have a very high standard of living in your country, and you have had an extraordinarily rapid increase in population. You have a very dense population, and have built up a maximum population on the assumption that your economic structure with its very large proportion of export trade and its great dependence on imported foodstuffs was a permanent structure. Cannot you see that it must be altered, and that your population in quantity and in distribution is wrong?" He says, "I do not say that you are going to do nothing to correct it, but you are applying all kinds of remedies at particular points, and you are not facing up to a change in fundamental conditions." In my judgment the foreigner generally overemphasizes this population question. He sees a million unemployed as a permanent minimum, and he nearly always ignores the fact that our industries, damaged, deranged and deflected as they were by war results, had really a rather remarkable absorbing power after the war. Up to about three years ago we were absorbing additional labour to the extent of about 100,000 to

1272961

150,000 people every year. As compared with the number of people employed before the war—let us look at that for the moment, rather than at the number unemployed—we had a full million extra people employed. We started with the results of dislocation at the end of the war to the extent of, say, a million people, and in the course of eight or nine years we employed an extra million people. That extra million was the annual crop of growth in the employable population. The job really set to industry was to find employment for two million people, the original million displaced by war conditions and the growing surplus every year amounting to another million. The task was to employ two million people, and we succeeded only to the extent of one-half. You may look upon that million either as the original displaced million who have been reabsorbed, and say that we failed to employ the increase in population, or you may put it the other way, and say we have employed the increase in population and failed to re-employ the original million. It comes to the same thing in the end, but it is always ignored that we did show remarkable recuperative powers in re-employing men. Despite the effect of rationalization and the difficulty of re-establishing export trade, we did achieve that much, and we are very rarely given credit for it. The foreigner also nearly always fails to estimate aright the damage done to the very delicate threads of our foreign trade by the consequences of the war, the effects upon our export markets in Russia and Germany and other places over a number of years, and the effect of various countries becoming more self-contained through the long interval of interrupted trade. We are very rarely given credit for the devastated area that we had to repair, the devastated area of trade. A physically devastated area which has been occupied by the enemy is obvious—it appeals to the eye and to the imagination. The other kind of devastated area requires greater economic sensibility to appreciate to the full.

The foreigner, of course, says that we did not set about our task in the right way—we did not recognize the new state of affairs, and tried by palliatives and local remedies to keep too long to the *status quo*. But if we are told that we tried for too long to keep up a standard of living which was relatively high compared with the standard of other peoples, we are entitled to ask whether, if we had reduced that standard, we should by that means have been able to employ *all* these people. The answer to that must be in the negative. A mere alteration of the standard of life would not have sufficed of itself—the dislocation was too far-reaching. André Siegfried, one of the most intelligent critics of our position, has said that what we have been suffering from is not a crisis, but a chronic malady, and that the way we go about it is characteristic of the

British. He says: "One cannot help remarking that England usually looks abroad first for the causes of her difficulties—always they are the fault of some-one else. If only this culprit or that would reform, then England might be able to regain her prosper-ity. It is magnificent, the way she can preach a ser-mon to the rest of the world, expose their weak-nesses, and point out their duties. She arouses the indignation of the countries who know how to behave against the scally-wags whose egotism blinds them to their international duties. A cynical French-man enjoys pointing out that when England says, 'You must think of others,' she really means, 'You must think of me.' Machiavellism? Not at all, simply rather naïve. Her instinct is to try to restore the conditions which suited her, instead of revising her own standards and adapting them to a world in which they are now out of place. French opinion is dumbfounded by such arguments, yet they are not met even in the most responsible circles. If one sug-gests that English wages are too high for competi-tion—very well, let the continental nations raise theirs; that the English working day is too short—reduce your own; that the English standard of liv-ing is pretentious—renounce your measly economy, civilize yourselves, be like us, learn how to live!"

That is a direct French criticism and one can find it repeated in a number of quarters, not merely in France, but in other countries. We are told that we are always looking abroad for the cause of our troubles. For the first two or three years after the war we were saying that things were not right because foreign markets were disturbed, and that when once Russia got right and the German economic organization was restored we should get back to normal conditions in international trade. Next, we are accused of talking about depreciated currencies and a perfect orgy of inflation in other countries, currencies dancing about, rates of exchange that could not be relied upon. It is impossible for us to do any trade requiring any credit attached to it, or any costing of manufactures ahead in such circumstances, and impossible with depreciated currencies to get a stable revival of trade. Next it is said that we complained of the inability or the refusal of some countries to work the Gold Standard. All this recrimination and all this talk about who works the Gold Standard and who does not is not really part of my subject, but it certainly comes under the head of diagnosis. The foreigner, rightly or wrongly, traces our sufferings to the fact that we have not had a proper degree of resiliency in our monetary and industrial conditions. He says that the trouble is that English manufacturing costs are among the highest in the world, and that we are not justified in having such high costs because individual output is not high enough to enable us to carry them. I do not want to do any injustice by my rendering of the foreign critics so I will read again what M. Siegfried says: "The evil from which England is suffering is that a whole section of the population is overpaid for its service, while the profits on capital are correspondingly diminished.

"That is the real cause of the trouble. When prices started to drop in 1921 owing to the rise of the pound sterling, nominal wages should have declined in proportion. If this adjustment had taken place, real wages would have been left intact, and the cost of production would have been relieved by the amount of the reduction. As England was not willing to reform, each increase in real wages actually became a direct increase in manufacturing costs, until a staggering burden was laid on the shoulders of the nation.

"The malady arises from many causes, all of which can be traced to a single germ. In a healthy economic structure, wages and prices, being retarded only by normal inertia, adjust themselves without difficulty. But in England there is also the social organization to contend with. The entire economic structure is frozen. No other community today is suffering to such an extent from this paralysis. Certain compartments in the national structure are isolated from the levelling influence of economic laws. The flexibility of retail prices is also considerably hampered, whereas in the case of wages the greater part seems to be rigidly pegged. The trade unions have imposed their point of view, and now every increase in wages, with the social progress involved, is considered a moral conquest for Labour that must not be given up at any price.

"As a result the workers have lost sight of the fact that wages, output and profits are all closely related. They contend that the nation owes them a certain wage, and that it is the owner's duty to pay it as best he can. England may be going through a serious crisis, but that does not move them in the least. In France we see nothing shameful in cutting down our standard of living, but to the Anglo-Saxon it is humiliating. This trade-union point of view is shared by the whole country, except, of course, the employers."

That is a common form of criticism from abroad, and it is our duty to examine how far it is a valid explanation of the position in which we find ourselves. This reliance upon the old British tradition, this suggestion that industry can bear to an unlimited extent any variation in the purchasing power of the pound sterling, this reliance on the maxim that "old England will pull through somehow," is something that the Latin mind finds it difficult to understand. On the other hand, we may find that their attitude of mind towards many questions is equally impossible to understand, and I am using the foreign critic only in order that we may try to see ourselves as others see us.

There is one rather interesting thing I must say in passing regarding those countries which have a definitely lower standard of living. It is said that we have in this country a character for domestic mismanagement, and that our housewives are not so thrifty or so careful—I wonder if these critics have ever been to Aberdeen—and they have to have more money given them for that reason. It is said that this necessitates the British workman getting a higher wage than is sufficient to make the French family happy, because the English housewife does not know how to make soup out of any conceivable object that has passed all other uses. How far it is possible to say that a standard of living or a level of wages is settled in highly competitive industrial conditions merely by domestic matters and requirements is a nice economic question. I would rather put it in this way; that if it be true that there is a differential between British and French domestic management, it seems to show that in France there is greater inertia in securing improvement or striving for improvement among people so situated.

Now I must deal with the very important theory put forward by a distinguished foreign economist regarding the influence of unemployment insurance on our economic problem. He thinks that high wages are a direct cause of unemployment, that is to say high *money* wages, and suggests that, with a falling price level which automatically increases real wages, we must have more unemployment. Not only do we automatically create unemployment, but we put another spoke in the machine because we pay a dole which we fix at a money rate that automatically becomes greater in real value as prices fall, and is so close to the bottom unskilled wage that we have a positive incentive to idleness. That is the contention, and it is buttressed or emphasized by elaborate statistical calculations of a very arresting character. Graphically it looks very convincing, but my own belief is that it is only a part of the truth, and that the situation as regards the creation of unemployment might be more easily met if the money dole fluctuated with the cost of living. A large part of the validity of the contention would be gone if we fixed the dole for the family not too close to the competitive unskilled wage-rate.

Then the criticism is made from America that so long as we have in our democracy a belief in an unlimited field of direct taxability, and so long as we think we can raid profits by taxation in order to support subsidies and remedies in every direction, so long shall we proceed on the downward path. There does seem to be some truth in that. Why are people employed, and how do they become employed? It is because someone brings together people with different capacities for labour and people with money saved from personal consumption, and employs these two classes of service in some scheme which will produce commodities at a price which will leave a margin above the rewards to those two agents. If he finds that the costs of production are so high that there is not sufficient margin to pay the wages demanded and the stipulated rate of interest on capital, then the employment never comes into being. The element of profit—I am not speaking of the ethics of it, but of the actual mechanism of it—is the mainspring of the expansion of employment in all countries of the world except Russia. That is a fact which we may as well recognize whether we like it or not. Everything that touches that element of profit has an important effect on the whole community. It is not merely a question of social justice. Anything which makes it more difficult to bring together these elements has an effect on the speed and the mechanism and the adjustment of the machine which provides employment. That is very elementary and very trite no doubt, but so unwelcome that it is often lost sight of.

Our American friend says that if we are not doing our best to look after the entrepeneur who is taking risks, if we are depressing and discouraging him, then the rest of the community will suffer. If, on the other hand, we are encouraging him, then we are on the way all of us to a share in a fuller national product. I would say to any full-blooded socialists present that the best thing you can do with the capitalist before you eat him is to fatten him well in your own interests, because you will have a better meal. Speaking quite seriously, I do say that to take everything you can squeeze out of that particular element which is actually the mainspring of present-day economic life may be in the long run a most short-sighted policy from the point of view of the total volume of the national product. The standard of living is not merely the fraction of the cake which you can eat and enjoy—it is the size of the cake that matters. Anything which hinders that size being as big as possible goes more to the root of the problem of distribution than our respective shares. This American criticism really means that so long as we go on paying out unlimited funds for balancing the Budget we shall never get right.

The immediate problem is the balance of trade, and how long a period will elapse before the crisis can end depends, it seems to me, upon the amount of attention which we give to this question. If it is regarded merely as a question of buying a hundred million sterling more than we are selling in goods and services, and having to make it right by an adjustment of the rate of exchange, we have not got to the root of the problem, for this "erroneous" balance of trade is not something to be compensated, it is something to be altered. Taking the position last autumn, there was probably a balance of something like two million pounds sterling a week on the wrong side—say at the rate of one hundred million sterling a year. Going farther back and considering the position at the beginning of the year 1931, when things were not so bad, I imagine you will find that over a whole year we have been somewhere about seventy-five million sterling on the wrong side apart from capital movements. We have to compare this with the old days when the balance was perhaps two hundred million sterling on the right side. At present, judging by the way in which the year finished in regard to physical exports and imports, and taking into account the diminished income from shipping and the fall in the yield of money investments abroad, I do not think that anyone can be so optimistic as to say that the position is materially better even after three months of depreciated currency. I know it is difficult to judge to what extent imports have risen by the forestalling of anticipated tariffs or revenue duties, but so far as one can tell we have not yet done anything substantially to correct this state of affairs. Of course we could go on quite a long while paying out this hundred million sterling provided it is recognized that we are living on capital. If we try to deal with that on the basis of short-term indebtedness we shall get into a very unstable position, and if we intend to do it on the basis of a permanent relinquishing of past savings we shall

have to face a new position entirely, because the
standard of living has been very materially affected
by the savings of previous generations. We have
been able to maintain our standard of living and to
pay for all our imports from abroad only because
two hundred million sterling a year was due to us
from foreign investments. If we eat into that fund
as we have been doing in the past ten years, using
more and more of that interest on foreign investments to pay for imports of food, and leaving less
and less for reinvestment, we shall have to face the
position that we shall soon have to encroach on
capital itself. We have to ask ourselves whether that
position is sufficiently serious to induce us to take
certain measures.

Let me deal now with an additional important
element in the balance of trade or payments which
is not usually associated in people's mind with that
balance. The balance of trade has been made definitely worse by the fall in prices and the redistribution of income that that fall has caused. If you
have thought about this, I am sure you will have
realized that every time the price level changes,
really the whole national income is redistributed.
People who are entitled to get money payments at
a fixed level, such as people who get interest on
War Loans and similar investments, may get more
of the total productivity of the country, and the
people not so entitled may get less. Therefore, any

change in the price level has an important effect in shifting the purchasing power of the country. I am not speaking of it at all as a question of social justice, but wish to draw attention to the fact that when purchasing power is shifted from one class of the community to another the direction in which that purchasing power is exercised changes. It is not exercised by the people who get it in exactly the same direction as it would have been if it had been retained by the people who lost it. If that occurs on any large scale it sets up a number of quite new tendencies. The fall in the price level has been such in the past two or three years as to make a difference in the total purchasing power of the country to the extent of one hundred and fifty or two hundred million sterling. That purchasing power is not now being exercised in the way in which it was exercised by the people who had it before. Different things are being bought, and it has expressed itself in such a way that it has directly or indirectly increased imports. Those people who have remained in employment, or who have remained in possession of their interest, have bought extra tins of attractively produced foodstuffs from abroad, have bought luxuries of one kind or another, have extended their road travels with imported petrol. In one way and another this alteration in prices and the alteration in the distribution of income does alter the direction of purchasing power. The national index of produc-

SIR JOSIAH STAMP

tion shows that in the past two years we had a fall
in physical production, apart from prices, of some
15 per cent. or more. What does purchasing power
consist of, when we view it with regard to buying
things from abroad, except our producing power in
this country? We can only buy from abroad the
equivalent of the wealth produced in this country
unless we are living on capital. If we are producing
more we have more to exchange and we can buy
more. We have had this fall in total production,
but during that same period, when we have had reduced purchasing power by 15 per cent., our actual
physical consumption of foreign imports has increased by 5 or 6 per cent., so that instead of going
down *pari passu* it has gone up. That illustrates the
point that there has been a new direction of purchasing power, and however unpleasant it may be
in its implications we have to face it. How are we
to get this right? In the next lecture Mr. Keynes
deals with the short-period remedy, and later lecturers deal with long-period remedies. But I am
bound to say that of the two classes of people, those
who rely entirely upon depreciated currency to do
it, and those who think that there must be some
other remedy before we can recover our equilibrium,
I think that the second are on the proper course. A
good deal depends on what the country will stand,
and on how much the country will understand.
When we are trying to get rid of past ideas and

THE WORLD'S ECONOMIC CRISIS

seeking to get new political ideas understood we are going away from the region of economics into the region of political psychology. There are those who would be content to rely on the advantage given by the depreciation of sterling. Ultimately, of course, the value of sterling must be the determinant, but there are so many capital adjustments going on, so many movements of liquid funds, so many things that may affect the price of sterling, that sterling may be higher or lower than the true position which it would occupy when these things have been cleared out of the way.

Personally I think the situation requires more drastic early treatment than the relief given by a depreciated pound, if we are to get the necessary check upon imports and the necessary impetus to exports. The position is all the more complicated when we consider the number of countries that are gradually getting into a similar position. I have not hesitated now to say for a period of more than eighteen months that although from the economic or production point of view I am a strong Free Trader, yet from the monetary point of view, and from the point of view of restoring the balance of trade, I want to see some definite discouragement, some definite artificial check to our vast volume of imports. That I believe to be a short-period remedy only. Nothing can alter the fact that in the long run exports and imports must be in equilibrium. One side of the balance of trade is not made up entirely of exports—there are important lending operations, but in my judgment there should be a check put on imports at the present time, and the effect left to work itself out in the lending operations. I am not prepared to put a definite time limit upon this short-term remedy, but I should imagine it might be perhaps for eighteen months to two years. I should despair of democracy if I thought that it must always hold in the future certain political ideas because they have existed in the past, for I do not see why an enlightened democracy cannot apply a short-period remedy if it understands exactly what is being done. If it is asked, When will that short-period remedy no longer be necessary? then I would say that in my judgment, if we got back to the price level of 1928–29 nobody is going to be really hurt, or unjustly treated. When by external or internal means we have got equilibrium, then I believe that short-period remedies of this kind can be relaxed. If it is said that short-period remedies of this type are politically impossible, then I am very sorry for democracy. Of course democracy and the politicians now are not exactly synonymous terms, but they are very closely associated.

Another point involved in the balance of trade that is extremely important is our shipping receipts. So long, of course, as the nations are looking to national self-sufficiency, and so long as high tariff walls are persisted in, our shipping earnings cannot be anything like what they might be, but as we gradually approach to greater freedom of trade our shipping earnings can revive. Whether we can ever completely reach world free trade I will not argue now, but the sooner we approach to that state of affairs the greater will be the total productivity of the world.

Another factor to take into account is the fifty or sixty million sterling that we have been earning through our great financial machine. Through our money market, our acceptance houses and discount houses, we have financed the international trade of the world, and that has earned us a lot of money which has played a very important part in feeding our huge population. When people say that these earnings are merely the profits of a few people in the City and do not concern them, they are quite wrong. These profits are an integral part of the balance of trade, and if they are destroyed, our task of reducing imports and restoring the balance of trade will be made even more difficult. One of the integral features in maintaining that profit is the integrity of sterling. An exporter in Java sends goods to Japan, and they cannot be turned into money for some time; but the exporter wants payment, and so the Japanese importer pays him by a ninety days bill. The importer in Japan promises to pay in three months, but the exporter in Java wants his money at once, and so takes that bill to his finance house, where it will be discounted by London eventually, and thus the Java exporter is able to carry on his transactions in the meantime before the bill matures. To carry on business of that kind you must have considerable knowledge of both parties. This business of bill discounting has to be carried on not only with intimate knowledge but with sustained courage. There are risks of all kinds of things happening in that three months. That type of business has been done here because the bill is drawn in sterling. Now if sterling does not mean the same thing this month as it meant last month, the exporter who has been given a bill will have difficulty in discounting it, for the finance house which takes it may find that although it is worth a certain sum when they accept it, it will be worth a very different sum when it matures. If sterling is not stable it must be a risky job. Of course there is a way of meeting that difficulty by the creation of a forward market in sterling exchange, but even if a forward market is created someone will have to take the risk of operations in sterling—it is shifted, but not destroyed. It is business which, as I say, requires great knowledge, and, to use colloquial slang, it also requires "guts." In certain money markets there is neither knowledge nor guts, for it is no good being extremely courageous one day and taking a lot of business, and then a few days later getting frightened by something, and trying to sell the bills and bonds at a huge discount. That is not the way to secure a world position in this kind of business. So, unless sterling remains very unreliable for a long period, long enough for other people to acquire the knowledge and calmness and equanimity necessary for such business, sterling will remain the chief currency of the world. It may fluctuate over long periods as it has done in the past without harm, and it will be only short-period fluctuations that will damage it. The City of London is not a mere machine grinding out money in a manner which is mysterious to many of us, but it is taking a commanding part in feeding our great population, and this matter of international finance is not one to which you and I can be indifferent.

I know there are many things upon which I have not touched at all, for it is quite impossible in one lecture to deal even lightly with everything. What I have tried to do is to focus attention on a general description of what is the most important problem of the day.

III

J. M. KEYNES

FROM WHO'S WHO (1932)

KEYNES, JOHN MAYNARD, M.A., C.B. 1917; F.B.A.; Fellow and Bursar of King's Coll., Camb.; Editor of Economic Journal since 1912; Secretary, Royal Economic Society; Member of Economic Advisory Council; Chairman, National Mutual Life Assurance Society; Officier de l'Ordre de Léopold; *b.* Cambridge, 5 June, 1883; *e.s.* of John Neville Keynes, *q. v.*, and Florence Ada, *d.* of late Rev. John Brown, D.D,; *m.* 1925, Lydia Lopokova. *Educ.:* Eton; King's College, Cambridge. Twelfth Wrangler, 1905; President of Cambridge Union Society, 1905; India Office, 1906–8; Treasury, 1915–19; Member of Royal Commission on Indian Finance and Currency, 1913–14; principal Representative of the Treasury at the Paris Peace Conference and Deputy for the Chancellor of the Exchequer on the Supreme Economic Council, Jan.–June, 1919; Member of Committee on Finance and Industry, 1929–31. *Publications:* Indian Currency and Finance, 1913; The Economic Consequences of the Peace, 1919; A Treatise on Probability, 1921; A Revision of the Treaty, 1922; A Tract on Monetary Reform, 1923; A Short View of Russia, 1925; The End of Laissez-Faire, 1926; A Treatise on Money, 2 vols., 1930.

III

J. M. KEYNES

I

THE immediate problem for which the world needs a solution to-day is different from the problem of a year ago. Then it was a question of how we could lift ourselves out of the state of acute slump into which we had fallen, and raise the volume of production and of employment back towards a normal figure. But to-day the primary problem is to avoid a far-reaching financial crisis. There is now no possibility of reaching a normal level of production in the near future. Our efforts are directed towards the attainment of more limited hopes. Can we prevent an almost complete collapse of the financial structure of modern capitalism? With no financial leadership left in the world and profound intellectual error as to causes and cures prevailing in the responsible seats of power, one begins to wonder and to doubt. At any rate, no one is likely to dispute that for the world as a whole the avoidance of financial collapse, rather than the stimulation of industrial activity, is now the front-rank problem. The restoration of industry must come second in order of time.

The immediate causes of the world financial panic —for that is what it is—are obvious. They are to be found in a catastrophic fall in the money value not only of commodities but of practically every kind of asset. The "margins," as we call them, upon confidence in the maintenance of which the debt and credit structure of the modern world depends have "run off." In many countries the assets of banks —perhaps in most countries with the exception of Great Britain—are no longer equal, conservatively valued, to their liabilities to their depositors. Debtors of all kinds find that their securities are no longer the equal of their debts. Few Governments still have revenues sufficient to cover the fixed money-charges for which they have made themselves liable.

Moreover, a collapse of this kind feeds on itself. We are now in the phase where the risk of carrying assets with borrowed money is so great that there is a competitive panic to get liquid. And each individual who succeeds in getting more liquid forces down the price of assets in the process, with the result that the margins of other individuals are impaired and their courage undermined. And so the process continues. It is perhaps in the United States that this has proceeded to the most incredible lengths. The collapse of values there has reached astronomical dimensions. Between January 1930 and September 1931 the market value of the common stocks listed on the New York Stock Exchange fell from $65,000 million to $45,000 million. One supposed that by that date the slump was far advanced. But the financial panic, as distinct from the industrial slump, was still to come. In the four months from September 1931 to January 1932 there was a further fall, equal in absolute amount to the former and in percentage amount much greater, namely from $47,000 million to $38,000 million. Yet this was perhaps the least part of the financial crash; for common stock values in America are notoriously volatile. The market value of bonds, which had not fallen at all between January 1930 and September 1931, declined in the next four months from $47,000 million to $38,000 million, that is to say, an *average* decline of 25 per cent. The fall in preferred stocks was greater still, and the position in real estate was not less serious. But the United States only offers an example, extreme owing to the psychology of its people, of a state of affairs which exists in some degree almost everywhere.

The competitive struggle for liquidity has now extended beyond individuals and institutions to nations and to governments, each of which endeavours to make its international balance sheet more liquid by restricting imports and stimulating exports by every possible means, the success of each one in this direction meaning the defeat of someone else. Moreover, every country discourages capital development within its own borders for fear of the effect on its international balance. Yet it will only be successful in its object in so far as its progress towards negation is greater than that of its neighbours.

We have here an extreme example of the *disharmony* of general and particular interest. Each nation, in an effort to improve its relative position, takes measures injurious to the absolute prosperity of its neighbours; and since its example is not confined to itself, it suffers more from similar action by its neighbours than it gains by such action itself. Practically all the remedies popularly advocated to-day are of this internecine character. Competitive wage-reductions, competitive tariffs, competitive liquidation of foreign assets, competitive currency deflations, competitive economy campaigns, competitive contractions of new development—all are of this beggar-my-neighbour description. The modern capitalist is a fair-weather sailor. As soon as a storm rises he abandons the duties of navigation and even sinks the boats which might carry him to safety by his haste to push his neighbours off and himself in.

I have spoken of competitive economy campaigns and competitive contractions of new development. But perhaps this needs a little more explanation. An

J. M. KEYNES

economy campaign, in my opinion, is a beggar-my-neighbour enterprise, just as much as competitive tariffs or competitive wage-reductions, which are perhaps more obviously of this description. For one man's expenditure is another man's income. Thus whenever we refrain from expenditure, whilst we undoubtedly increase our own margin, we diminish that of someone else; and if the practice is universally followed, everyone will be worse off. An individual may be forced by his private circumstances to curtail his normal expenditure, and no one can blame him. But let no one suppose that he is performing a public duty in behaving in such a way. An individual or an institution or a public body, which voluntarily and unnecessarily curtails or postpones expenditure which is admittedly useful, is performing an anti-social act.

Unfortunately the popular mind has been educated away from the truth, away from common sense. The average man has been taught to believe what his own common sense, if he relied on it, would tell him was absurd. Even remedies of a right tendency have become discredited because of the failure of a timid and vacillating application of them at an earlier stage.

Now, at last, under the teaching of hard experience, there may be some slight movement towards wiser counsels. But through lack of foresight and constructive imagination the financial and political authorities of the world have lacked the courage or the conviction at each stage of the decline to apply the available remedies in sufficiently drastic doses; and by now they have allowed the collapse to reach a point where the whole system may have lost its resiliency and its capacity for a rebound.

Meanwhile the problem of reparations and war debts darkens the whole scene. We all know that these are now as dead as mutton, and as distasteful as stale mutton. There is no question of any substantial payments being made. The problem has ceased to be financial and has become entirely political and psychological. If in the next six months the French were to make a very moderate and reasonable proposal in final settlement, I believe that the Germans, in spite of all their present protestations to the contrary, would accept it and would be wise to accept it. But to all outward appearances the French mind appears to be hardening against such a solution and in favour of forcing a situation in which Germany will default. French politicians are feeling that it will be much easier for them, *vis-à-vis* the home political front, to get rid of reparations by a German default than to reach by agreement a moderate sum, most of which might have to be handed on to the United States. Moreover, this outcome would have what they deem to be the advantage of piling up grievances and a legal case against Germany for use in connection with the other outstanding questions created between the two countries by the Treaty of Versailles. I cannot, therefore, extract much comfort or prospective hope from developments in this sphere of international finance.

II

Well, I have painted the prospect in the blackest colours. What is there to be said on the other side? What elements of hope can we discern in the surrounding gloom? And what useful action does it still lie in our power to take?

The outstanding ground for cheerfulness lies, I think, in this—that the system has shown already its capacity to stand an almost inconceivable strain. If anyone had prophesied to us a year or two ago the actual state of affairs which exists to-day, could we have believed that the world could continue to maintain that even degree of normality which we actually have? Could anyone, knowing the present level of commodity prices, have believed that the great majority of the debtor countries producing raw materials would still be meeting their obligations? Could anyone, told the present prices of bonds in the United States, have supposed that the banks and Stock Exchanges of that country could still keep their doors open? Could anyone, inside or outside of Germany, have believed beforehand that Germany could have stood such a degree of economic and financial pressure as she is now suffering, without a collapse of her political and social organization? This remarkable capacity of the system to take punishment is the best reason for hoping that we still have time to rally the constructive forces of the world.

Moreover, there has been a still recent and, in my judgment, most blessed event, of which we have not yet had time to gain the full benefit. I mean Great Britain's abandonment of the Gold Standard. I believe that this event has been charged with beneficent significance over a wide field. If Great Britain had somehow contrived to maintain her gold parity, the position of the world as a whole to-day would be considerably more desperate than it is, and default more general.

For Great Britain's action has had two signal consequences. The first has been to stop the decline of prices, measured in terms of national currencies, over a very considerable proportion of the world. Consider for a moment what an array of countries are now linked to the fortunes of sterling rather than of gold. Australasia, India, Ceylon, Malaya, East and West Africa, Egypt, Ireland and Scandinavia; and, in substance though not so literally, South America, Canada and Japan. Outside Europe there are no countries in the whole world except South Africa and the United States which now conform to a Gold Standard. France and the United

States are the only remaining countries of major importance where the Gold Standard is functioning freely.

This means a very great abatement of the deflationary pressure which was existing six months ago. Over wide areas producers are now obtaining prices in terms of their domestic currencies which are not so desperately unsatisfactory in relation to their costs of production and to their debts. These events have been too recent to attract all the attention they deserve. There are several countries of which it could be argued that their economic and financial condition may have turned the corner in the last six months. It is true, for example, of Australia. I think it may be true of Argentine and Brazil. There has been an extraordinary improvement in India, where one consequence of the discount of sterling in terms of gold, which no one predicted, has almost solved the financial problem of the Government—I mean the export of gold previously hoarded. Already in the four months since October 1931, £36 million has been exported; and the export is now proceeding, and seems likely to continue, at the rate of above £1 million a week. As regards Great Britain herself, the rest of the world, and even we ourselves perhaps, may have a little overlooked the change since last September, which represents, if not an absolute, at least a relative, improvement. The number of persons employed to-day is not less than the number employed a year ago, which is true of no other industrial country. The present actual rate of expenditure on the unemployed falls well below the Budget provision. This has been achieved in spite of the fact that there has been, even during the past year, a further rise in real wages; for whilst money wages have fallen by 2 per cent., the cost of living, in spite of the depreciation of the sterling exchange, has fallen by 4 per cent. And the explanation is an encouragement for the future. For the explanation lies in the fact that over a wide field of her characteristic activities Great Britain to-day is once again the cheapest producer in the world. I believe that our textile industries can now produce more cheaply than their chief competitors over a wide range of qualities. I believe that we can run ships to-day at a lower cost than anyone else. I believe that we have an opportunity of making a bid for the best part of the world's export trade in motor-cars and motor-lorries. All this will tell increasingly with time. The forces set on foot last September have by no means had time as yet to work their full effect. But even to-day Great Britain is decidedly the most prosperous country in the world.

Perhaps you will retort that hopes based on .an improvement in Great Britain's competitive position are inconsistent with what I was saying a few minutes ago about the uselessness of one country gaining at the expense of another. You may also think it an inconsistency with what I was saying then that I should have advocated a protective tariff for this country last year and am not prepared to oppose it to-day with any heat of conviction. The explanation is to be found in my belief that it is a necessary preliminary to world recovery that this country should regain its liberty of action and its power of international initiative. I believe, further, that we and we alone can be trusted to use that power of initiative, when once we have regained it, to the general advantage. I agree with those who think that many of the difficulties of recent years were due to the fact that the creditor balance available to finance new international investment had largely passed out of our hands into the hands of France and the United States. And I therefore welcome, and indeed require as an indispensable preliminary to a world recovery, that there should be a material strengthening of the creditor position of Great Britain.

It would not be true to say, in spite of these favourable developments, that there is as yet in any part of the world an adequate relaxation of the deflationary pressure. But the widespread abandonment of the Gold Standard is preparing the way for the possibility of such a relaxation. Moreover, I consider it not unlikely that further currencies will join the sterling group in the course of 1932; in particular South Africa, Germany and the Central European countries, and quite possibly (in spite of their present determination to the contrary) Holland dragged at the heels of Java which will find economic life under the Gold Standard increasingly impracticable.

But there is a second major consequence of the partition of the countries of the world into two groups on and off the Gold Standard respectively. For the two groups as they now are, or as they soon may be, roughly correspond to those which have been exercising deflationary pressure on the rest of the world by having a *net* creditor position which causes them to draw gold and those which have been suffering this pressure. Now the departure of the latter group from gold means the beginning of a process towards the restoration of economic equilibrium. It means the setting into motion of natural forces which are certain in course of time to undermine and eventually destroy the creditor position of the two leading creditor gold countries.

The process will be seen most rapidly in the case of France, whose creditor position is likely to be completely undermined before the end of 1932. The cessation of reparation receipts, the loss of tourist traffic, the competitive disadvantage of her export trades with non-gold countries, and the importation of a large proportion of the world's available gold will, between them, do the work. And, when the last gold bar in the world has been safely lodged in the Bank of France, that will be the appropriate moment for the German Government to announce that one of their chemists has just perfected his technique for making the stuff at 6d. an ounce.

In the case of the United States the process may be a slower one, largely because the reduction of tourist traffic, which costs France so dear, means for the United States a large saving. But the tendency will be the same. A point will surely come when the current release of gold from India and from the mines will exceed the favourable balance of the gold countries.

The undermining of the competitive position of the export industries of these gold countries will be, in truth, in response to their own request; or, at any rate, a case of poetic justice. The rest of the world owes them money. They will not take payment in goods; they will not take it in bonds; they have already received all the gold there is. The puzzle which they have set to the rest of the world admits logically of only one solution, namely that some way must be found of doing without their exports. The expedient of continually reducing world prices failed; for prices were dragged down equally everywhere. But the expedient of exchange depreciation relatively to gold will succeed.

Thus a process has been set moving which may

relieve in the end the deflationary pressure. The question is whether this will have time to happen before financial organization and the system of international credit break under the strain. If they do, then the way will be cleared for a concerted policy, probably under the leadership of Great Britain, of capital expansion and price raising throughout the world. For without this the only alternative solution which I can envisage is one of the general default of debts and the disappearance of the existing credit system, followed by rebuilding on quite new foundations.

The following, then, is the chapter of events which might conceivably—I will not attempt to evaluate the probability of their occurrence—lead us out of the bog. The Financial Crisis might wear itself out before a point of catastrophe and general default had been reached. This is perhaps happening. The greatest dangers may have been surmounted during the past few months. *Pari passu* with this, the deflationary pressure exerted on the rest to the world by the unbalanced creditor position of France and the United States may be relaxed, through their losing their creditor position, as a result of the steady operation of the forces which I have already described. If and when these things are clearly the case, we shall then enter the cheap money phase. This is the point at which, on the precedent of previous slumps, we might hope for the beginning of recovery. The end of deflationary pressure will show itself in a firm tendency for the sterling exchange. We should use this strength to cheapen money and increase the volume of credit, to restart home activity and to lend abroad to the utmost of our powers. For the impulse to world recovery will have to come from us in the first instance, and not from the United States.

I am not confident, however, that on this occasion the cheap money phase will be sufficient by itself to bring about an adequate recovery of new investment. Cheap money means that the riskless, or supposedly riskless, rate of interest will be low. But actual enterprise always involves some degree of risk. It may still be the case that the lender, with his confidence shattered by his experiences, will continue to ask for new enterprise rates of interest which the borrower cannot expect to earn. Indeed this was already the case in the moderately cheap money phase which preceded the financial crisis of last autumn.

If this proves to be so, there will be no means of escape from prolonged and perhaps interminable depression except by direct State intervention to promote and subsidize new investment. Formerly there was no expenditure out of the proceeds of borrowing, which it was thought proper for the State to incur, except war. In the past, therefore, we have not infrequently had to wait for a war to terminate a major depression. I hope that in the future we shall not adhere to this purist financial attitude, and that we shall be ready to spend on the enterprises of peace what the financial maxims of the past would only allow us to spend on the devastations of war. At any rate I predict with an assured confidence that the only way out is for us to discover *some* object which is admitted even by the deadheads to be a legitimate excuse for largely increasing the expenditure of someone on something!

In all our thoughts and feelings and projects for the betterment of things, we should have it at the back of our heads that this is not a crisis of poverty but a crisis of abundance. It is not the harshness and the niggardliness of nature which is oppressing us, but our own incompetence and wrong-headedness which hinders us from making use of the bountifulness of inventive science and causes us to be overwhelmed by its generous fruits. The voices which— in such a conjuncture—tell us that the path of escape is to be found in strict economy and in refraining, wherever possible, from utilizing the world's potential production, are the voices of fools and madmen. There is a passage from David Hume in which he says:

"Though the ancients maintained, that in order to reach the gift of prophecy, a certain divine fury or madness was requisite, one may safely affirm

[72]

that, in order to deliver such prophecies as these, no more is necessary than merely to be in one's senses free from the influence of popular madness and delusion."

It is a high social duty to-day for everyone to use his influence, whatever it may be, in private and in public, in favour of every kind of expansion and expenditure, which is financially possible to those who incur it, and which in better times would be generally admitted to be legitimate and useful.

Obviously it is much more difficult to solve the problem to-day than it would have been a year ago. But I still believe even now, as I believed then, that we still could be, if we would, the masters of our fate. The obstacles to recovery are not material. They reside in the state of knowledge, judgment, and opinion of those who sit in the seats of authority. Unluckily the traditional and ingrained beliefs of those who hold responsible positions throughout the world grew out of experiences which contained no parallel to the present, and are often the opposite of what one would wish them to believe to-day.

In France the weight of authoritative opinion and public sentiment is genuinely and sincerely opposed to the whole line of thought which runs through what I have been saying. They think that if everyone had behaved as they have, everyone would have as much gold as they have. Their own accumulations are the reward of virtue, and the losses which the rest of us have suffered are the penalty of imprudence. They wish to go on to the grim conclusion. There is nothing to do with them but to wait for their conversion by the grinding pressure of events; though they are by nature such realists in the last resort that when the proof of experience arrives they may be unexpectedly exempt from obstinacy. In the United States it is almost inconceivable what rubbish a public man has to utter to-day if he is to keep respectable. Serious and sensible bankers, who as men of common sense are trying to do what they can to stem the tide of liquidation and to stimulate the forces of expansion, have to go about assuring the world of their conviction that there is no serious risk of inflation, when what they really mean is that they cannot yet see good enough grounds for daring to hope for it. In this country opinion is probably more advanced. I believe that the ideas of our statesmen and even of our bankers are on much sounder lines than those current elsewhere. What we have to fear here is timidity and a reluctance to act boldly. When once we have regained a power of initiative we must use it without hesitation or delay for expanding purchasing power ourselves and for helping others to expand. *We* must set the example. We must believe that safety lies in boldness and nowhere else. If we lack boldness and use our strength, when it begins to return to us, to consolidate our position, as the phrase goes, which means in practice assuming in our turn the rôle of deflating the rest of the world, then I recur to those prognostications of gloom with which I opened my remarks.

IV

SIR BASIL BLACKETT

FROM WHO'S WHO (1932)

BLACKETT, SIR BASIL PHILLOTT, K.C.B., *cr.* 1921; K.C.S.I., *c.* 1926; C.B. 1915; a Director of the Bank of England; Chairman, Imperial and International Communications Ltd.; Director of Cables and Wireless Ltd., of Eastern and Associated Telegraph Companies, of Marconi's Wireless Telegraph Co. Ltd.; Director of De Beers Ltd.; President, British Social Hygiene Council; Chairman of Colonial Development Advisory Committee; *b.* 8 Jan., 1882; *s.* of late Rev. William Russell Blackett, M.A., Vicar of Holy Trinity Church, Nottingham, 1885–91; *m.* 1920, Beatrice, *d.* of late Edward H. Bonner, New York. *Educ.:* Marlborough; University College, Oxford. M.A., 1st Class Lit. Hum. 1904; entered Treasury, 1904; Secretary to Indian Finance and Currency Commission, 1913–14, and to Capital Issues Committee, 1915; went on special mission to U.S.A. Government, Oct. 1914, in connection with exchange problems arising out of the war; Member of Anglo-French Financial Mission to U.S.A. which raised the Anglo-French Loan of 500,000,000 dollars, October 1915; Member of National War Savings Committee, 1916; Representative of British Treasury in U.S.A., 1917–19; Controller of Finance, Treasury, 1919–22; Finance Member of the Executive Council of the Governor-General of India, 1922–28; Commendatore of the Order of the Crown of Italy; Officer Legion of Honour.

IV

SIR BASIL BLACKETT

Sir Arthur Salter and Sir Josiah Stamp have analysed the world crisis. Mr. Keynes has followed with an examination of the immediate position and what is immediately possible. All have given us something of their views as to the way of escape, but have left this part of the subject to be developed in later lectures.

In these circumstances it is neither needful nor desirable that I should occupy your attention with further analysis of the causes and history of the world crisis. My aim will be to look ahead and deal with the longer outlook.

A fair summary of what has been expressed in previous lectures would be that modern civilization finds itself on the brink of chaos owing to the inability of human beings to manage the machine they have brought into being. It is not merely that we are failing to make full use of the marvellous opportunities which Science opens up to the twentieth century. We are in immediate danger of becoming the victims of a Frankenstein monster of our own creation; the genius of man has outstripped his code of morals both in the national and in the international sphere. The structure of the twentieth century cannot be built up on outworn foundations. If we are to survive we must be prepared to "think adventurously" and to challenge existing values and the customs based on them, carefully distinguishing between those that have passed their usefulness and those that are really essential. At the same time we cannot hope to escape by ignoring the present and the past, whose children we are—the inheritors of a thousand-year-old civilization. We cannot preserve and hand on to our successors the achievements of the spirit of man in the long ages of human history if we conceive of our task as a violent break with the past. Both bloody revolution and a policy of drift lead alike to a new Dark Ages.

Though not all of the six lecturers in this series would claim or admit the description of ourselves as economists, we are all of us interested in economic questions, and we have no doubt been brought together with the expectation that our angle of approach to our subject will be economic. I freely admit, however, that economic measures alone, however far-reaching, will not solve all our problems, and that it is rather to the growth of a higher human mentality and the attainment of a higher spirituality, more worthy of the scientific achievements of our age, that I look for true emancipation. Life will never be worth living under an economic system, however admirable, which does not take account of ethical and æsthetic values. Sir Arthur Salter, in a moving peroration which made an immense impression on all who heard it, spoke of the need for magnanimity in international dealings. Magnanimity, greatness of soul, and courage, greatness of heart, are indeed the twin keys to the door of escape.

The war and its aftermath provide obvious explanations for most of the world's present troubles, but it is possible that we overestimate their importance as fundamental causes. The war itself was in some sense only a devastating explosion of forces which in the passage from the nineteenth to the twentieth century were being inexorably generated by the conflict between man's rapid intellectual and scientific advance and his slow mental and spiritual growth. The war hastened the *tempo* of the drama and has intensified its bitterness and its tragedy: but there are many elements in present-day economic conditions which would anyhow have led to maladjustment. As examples, I would point to the progressive decline in the birth-rate and in the death-rate and in the growth of population of the countries where Western civilization was most advanced, the impact of Western civilization on Africa and on Asia, and the growing instability of capital due to applied science and new invention. The philosophy of *laisser-faire* in the nineteenth century assumed a rapid growth of population and of material progress, a wide area outside Europe for expansion and new development, and something approaching permanent stability of value for such things as railways and coal-mines and in general for capital works involving heavy long-term outlay. Obsolescence of plant and obsolescence of skilled labour on the scale to which we have painfully begun to try to accustom ourselves in recent years was not provided for in the Victorian industrial outlook. Who, for instance, foresaw the onslaught of the internal-combustion engine and road transport upon the railway systems of the world, the sudden destruction of the earning power of the South Wales coal-mining valleys, the conversion of prosperous regions of our north-east coast into derelict areas? With the possibility continually present of some new invention which will throw on the scrap-heap the whole of the factory buildings and plant and accumulated experience and skill engaged in an industry, it is not want of enterprise alone, but foresight and caution that may be very fully justified, which prevent capital from flowing freely into channels which on a short view promise glittering prospects. Suppose for example that the conveyance of electric power by wireless were suddenly to be proved not only theoretically but commercially feasible, what would be the fate of the capital which we as a nation have—very wisely as we think—sunk in our nation-wide electricity schemes, and what would happen to the industry of manufacturing power cables? When we let our minds dwell on this aspect of modern life we are tempted to sigh for Samuel Butler's *Erewhon* and to endorse the well-known paradox of one of our Bishops who said it would be a good thing for the world if Science took a twenty years' holiday from invention.

Internationally again *laisser-faire,* which at no time obtained as undisputed a sway over the practices of Governments and Parliaments as it did over the minds of economic professors, has finally been bankrupted by political nationalism. Unrestricted Free Trade, for example, has never made the slightest appeal to our fellow-citizens in the Dominions. Whether they were of our own blood, as in Australia or of different race as in India, they were very naturally not content to perpetuate the *status quo* which meant that they must confine themselves to primary production and forgo the power to provide openings for their sons in any of the skilled professions and occupations which go with the manufacturing industries. Fatal to human progress as are the high tariff walls of to-day, it has long been obvious that the philosophy of *laisser-faire* has no answer to the reasoned demand for wider opportunities and a balanced economic life for large new communities overseas and for highly self-conscious national groups in old Europe.

The mere growth in size of the units of productive industry leading to enormous aggregations, such as Imperial Chemical Industries—to take a prominent example from this country—has further served to render invalid many of the basic assumptions of the nineteenth century regarding mobility of labour and fluidity of capital. A large concern in which huge sums have been sunk in bricks and mortar and plant may be forced to go on producing at an economic loss by the sheer force of its momentum or by the magnitude of the human disasters which would accompany stoppage. The spread of the technique of trade-union organization and side by side with it the increase of humanitarian and social conscience regarding problems of housing, health, sanitation, and working conditions generally, have rendered impossible or inadmissible many of those brutal economic adjustments which our grandfathers were able to regard as due to the intervention of a wise providence, which used enlightened self-interest and unregulated human competitiveness as its mysterious means to perform wonders in the cause of moral and material progress.

In the economic sphere, then, the first necessity for the building up of the twentieth century is a new philosophy to take the place of the doctrine of *laisser-faire*. Unfortunately for us in Britain, the political prejudices of three generations have identified the doctrine of *laisser-faire* with the cause of Free Trade in the fiscal controversy between Free

Trade and Protection. To many among the more advanced social and political thinkers and workers the fight for Free Trade has taken on the aspect of a struggle for the wider interests of humanity against a selfish nationalistic or imperialistic greed and acquisitiveness leading to war and aggression which had become equated in their minds with the demand for tariffs and protection. That this identification was and is incorrect can easily be proved by the pertinent fact that *laisser-faire* has held and holds the field in all matters outside the particular question of tariffs far more strongly in the United States than in Britain. If tariffs here at long last win the day against Free Trade in this country it is not because the nation has been converted to Protectionism but because tariffs may well be a useful instrument in a consciously controlled reconstruction of our economic life, and because we have realized that the whole body of *laisser-faire* doctrine, the undiluted individualistic philosophy of Bentham and his school, has broken down, is dead, and ought to be buried.

What are we to put in its place? We look abroad and see in Italy and in Russia two very different political systems actively engaged in attempting to rebuild their national life on new foundations. Diametrically opposed in many important respects, Fascism and Bolshevism are agreed on two points. They both pay scant respect to the claims of politi-

cal and personal freedom. They both insist on the
need for conscious corporative direction and forward planning in their economic activities. If we are
abundantly right, as we believe we are, in continuing to assert that freedom is and always must be a
supreme human value without which life is worth-
less, have we any sound reason for denying their
assertion that conscious corporative direction and
forward planning are essential to the reconstruction
of twentieth-century economic life? A year ago
planning was a new and startling idea in this country. To-day it has become a cliché and is correspondingly devoid of content to most of us; but I think
it is still true to say that, rooted as we are in British
traditions of personal and political freedom, the
average man and woman among us instinctively dis-
trusts the idea of conscious corporative planning,
and we tremble for our cherished privileges and
liberty when it is suggested that we have something
to learn from Italy and Russia. Nevertheless it is
instructive and heartening to observe that the cry
of interference with the rights of property and with
individual freedom has failed to make any impression when raised against the Town and Country
Planning Bill recently reintroduced by the National
Government in the House of Commons, and that so
far at any rate the London Passenger Transport Bill
seems to have survived the onslaught of its individualistic enemies.

SIR BASIL BLACKETT

I wish to put before you this evening the view that conscious corporative planning is not only a desirable means of progress but an unavoidable necessity if we are to save the economic structure of modern civilization from disaster, and that the immediate task to which we should bend all our energies is to prove to ourselves and to the world that planning is consistent with freedom and freedom with planning.

The task of steering a wise course between tyrannous compulsion and anarchic individualism is not an easy one. The community does already intervene actively in the life of the individual in very many ways, whether as the State or as the Local Authority, or simply to assist groups to do collectively for the community what as individuals they could not achieve in isolation. Perhaps the building up of a body of statutory law and of custom, and of a code of behaviour for the motorist, is as good an example as can be found of the manner in which we are trying to solve new problems. In the absence of statutory control and of the road users' code of behaviour, we should find ourselves hopelessly frustrated and far less free than we are when we motor along country roads or city streets. We have enhanced our freedom by co-operative action and ready compliance with rules which are in a true sense self-imposed. The freedom which we seek to save and to enhance is clearly something different from the right to do as we like. We are wisely extending the spirit of the mediæval doctrine of Eminent Domain to spheres other than the use of land.

In this connection there is much in the great address of the Prince of Wales at the meeting of the National Council of Service on January 27th on Youth and Social Service which is admirably attuned to the needs of to-day.

"You should not think of social service purely as State action . . . nor only as the wonderful voluntary work which is being done in connection with the countless good causes throughout the country. . . . We must realize that the amenities of life, like its essentials, are best secured by the personal effort and individual contribution of every member of the community, and are not a sort of heaven-sent manna to be garnered and enjoyed without effort, service, or obligation."

The Prince of Wales was calling for planned social effort by the individual, and it is significant that his emphasis was laid on the fact that such social effort has to be consciously organized and planned if it is to be of any use to the community. We are far from the unregulated individualism of the nineteenth century. Never in the world's history has there been so large and widespread a fund of human good will among men and women all over the world anxious to serve their generation, and never have men and women felt more keenly the exasperating frustration which renders their good intentions and desires nugatory and unavailing. Our ideal is a nation and a world of free men and women self-disciplined by an active social conscience, and if we are to go forward towards our ideal we must both have a comprehensive map and plan consciously in mind to guide all our steps, and must willingly accept the duty and obligation of framing and keeping rules of the road, compulsory where compulsion is needed to protect ourselves against the road-hog, but voluntary in the sense that they are imposed and observed by our own conscious volition and corporate action.

This country has always been inclined to pride itself on muddling through. It has had a perfectly valid sense of the futility of grandiose paper plans which break down at the first attempt to put them into practice, and an obscure feeling that it is better to take the next practical step in one particular field without worrying overmuch as to what comes after, or even as to the parallel steps in other parts of the field which are necessary to make what it is doing really effective or even worth doing. There is, however, all the difference in the world between building an ideal State or planning Utopia and consciously and deliberately thinking out a plan of national reconstruction in all its interrelations, with a Time and Progress Schedule designed to keep advance in each part of the front in step with the general advance along the whole line. Moreover, while what is practicable within the next decade or half-decade must depend on the feasibility of carrying the practical man and woman along and on the successful application of the technique of persuasion to a somewhat stubborn mass of public opinion, nevertheless there is great value in having a comprehensive vision of the whole field as we should like to see it—as it were a timeless picture—and a long-term objective for a period ten, fifteen, twenty or more years ahead. If the leaders have a comprehensive view of the whole and a clear picture, even if only in the broadest outline, of the England they would like to see a generation ahead, they will be in a position as never heretofore to assess the value and the relative priority of any particular measure of reform, and to make sure that it is in general not out of place and not out of step with the comprehensive plan for which they are working.

First and foremost, then, in the planning of national reconstruction comes the necessity for comprehensive insight and a firm grasp of the interrelationships between the various aspects of our political and economic and social life. The Cabinet Room in 10 Downing Street ought to have prominently emblazoned on its walls the Hegelian motto: "The Altogetherness of Everything." How many of our troubles are due to our insistence on thinking and acting piecemeal? And as a natural corollary to our adopting and acting on two or more inconsistent policies simultaneously? At the present moment Tariffs, Currency Policy, Reparations, Inter-Allied Debts, Foreign Policy, Imperial Policy, Disarmament, Rationalization of Industry, Town and Country Planning, Unemployment, Derelict Areas, Transport, Electricity Distribution, are inextricably inter-related. How far are they being considered in close connection with each other? A year ago we had the Macmillan Committee sitting with terms of reference which prevented it from considering alternatives to the Gold Standard, and to-day the Unemployment Committee is at work preparing a Final Report which unless it goes outside its terms of reference will have nothing to say about reparation or tariffs or the stabilization of the purchasing power of money. It is a common gibe against the expert that he knows more and more about less and less. He must in common fairness be given the opportunity at least of pointing out that the cleaning up of his field will be useless or even harmful if thistles continue to flourish in those which lie all round him.

Nothing, for example, has been more heart-rending in the past decade than the way in which every kind of effort towards world recovery and reconstruction, both national and international, has been rendered abortive, often after showing great initial promise of success, by the catastrophic fall in the purchasing power of money. Here we come to the heart of our present-day problem of a financial and economic crisis brought on not by scarcity but by plenty. It is the fact that this is a crisis of plenty which has shocked mankind and accounts in a special degree for that intense interest in economic and currency questions which has among its other manifestations brought crowded audiences to listen to these lectures.

It is said that in proportion to their numbers there are more chess experts in the lunatic asylums than any other class, and next to them come currency experts. In view of what we have done with currency and currency has done with us in the last twenty years, we are all of us fit for the lunatic asylum. If many currency experts go mad, it is the natural result of their coming face to face with the insanity of the monetary systems with which man has tortured himself ever since he passed from barter to money. Money was meant to be a yardstick with which to measure the value to be put on commodities and services in process of being exchanged for each other, but throughout the ages mankind has never been able to devise a monetary yardstick which did not at one time measure an inch and at another a hundred or more inches. Let me give you one set of figures as an example. Between April 1, 1920, and April 1, 1931, the nominal deadweight debt of Great Britain fell from £7,829 millions to

£7,413 millions. During the same period the Statist Index of Wholesale Prices fell from 295 to 101. Therefore the 1920 debt of £7,829 millions was worth £2,680 millions at 1931 prices, while the debt of £7,413 millions in 1931 was worth £7,413 millions. Even in 1924, when the debt was nominally £7,641 millions, its value in terms of 1931 commodities was only £4,708 millions. Now although it is obviously not the fact that money remains stable in terms of commodities, nearly everything we do in our everyday business life is based on the unconscious assumption that it does remain approximately stable. That is true of every insurance or other money contract we enter into, every wage-rate that is fixed over a period of months, every lease, every mortgage, every public issue of bonds or debentures or Government Stock. Our Trustee Acts in their endeavour to protect the widow and orphan make it impossible for a trustee to take fluctuations in the purchasing power of money into account and insist on his investing in Government Stocks and similar securities, which, when money values are as unstable as of late, is about the most unsatisfactory form of gambling conceivable.

In the forefront of the reforms which the planned twentieth century demands is a stable money whose purchasing power will remain constant. It is to our failure to seize this primary necessity of any rational monetary system that our present distress is preeminently to be attributed. And we have erred with our eyes open. At the Genoa Conference of 1922 some forty-five nations there assembled solemnly adopted a series of financial resolutions which set before the world two principal aims, first the restoration of the Gold Standard and second the prevention of fluctuations in the purchasing power of gold. The nations of the world were remarkably successful in giving effect to the first part of these recommendations, and by 1929 practically the whole world except China was on the Gold Standard. But they signally failed to give effect to the second part of these recommendations, the stabilization of the purchasing power of gold, although it was far the more important of the two. Indeed it may be averred that the return to gold was by itself of importance mainly as a step towards stability of prices. By this neglect we have earned the well-deserved punishment of our present distress. We snatched at stability of the foreign exchanges on the basis of an international Gold Standard, whose main value was that it would facilitate and expand world trade. With poetic justice most of the nations which have remained nominally on the Gold Standard are moving heaven and earth to restrict world trade in order not to be driven off the Gold Standard.

Amid the many discouraging signs of the times there is some comfort in the reflection that all over the world, and in particular in this country, there are growing evidences of a widespread determination to have done with the absurdities of violently fluctuating price levels and to insist on a monetary system which is worthy of the twentieth century. In passing, I should like to add a word as to the extraordinary capacity which people in this country have shown to keep calm amid the financial panic which has led in almost every other part of the world to unreasoned hoarding of gold and of notes, with all the consequent dangers. The way in which the taxpayer has come forward to pay his income-tax is another evidence of British character under difficulties. I see more hope for salvation from chaos in these proofs of British character than in any other factor in the present situation.

There is still a strong tendency to stigmatize all talk about stable money as unorthodox, visionary, cranky. Do not be frightened. Let the British people with their strong grasp of the practical realize that stable money is an intensely practical proposition, within their grasp to-day, if only they will believe in it and work for it and insist on getting it, and make up their minds to accept and enforce all the measures necessary to secure and maintain it.

I cannot on this occasion go deeper into the technicalities involved, which are many and difficult. In saying that stable money is practicable and attainable, I do not mean that it is easy and simple of attainment. But it is surely worth a big effort to attain it.

Before leaving the subject of stable money I wish, however, to deal with one aspect of it which seems to cause real difficulty to many people. By stability of the price level I do not mean that particular prices will never vary, that there will always be the same fixed price for a loaf of bread or for a pair of boots of given quality. The price we pay for a commodity or service is expressed in money, but money is really only a simplified means of expressing and facilitating the exchange of one commodity or service for another commodity or service. If I say that my wages are £3 per week and an umbrella costs ten shillings, what I mean is that my weekly wages are worth six umbrellas. I express in terms of money the value in exchange between my week's work and an umbrella. Relative prices will always vary. The price of wheat should go down in terms of boots or umbrellas in a year of good harvests. If the amount of human effort required to produce and market a pair of boots is reduced by increased efficiency or a new invention, their price relatively to other things will go down. Their price will also go down in relation to wages generally, including the wages of those who make and market boots. With stable money there will be a natural tendency for the price, that is the remuneration for services, including wages, to increase in relation to the price or cost of commodities.

Many people object, when one talks of stable prices, that efforts to fix prices or to valorize commodities have always failed. The answer is that we are not talking about fixing particular prices but about stabilizing the purchasing power of money over goods and services generally. This answer often leads to a second objection—Why should prices not go down as methods of production improve and less human effort is absorbed in producing things? Here again is a confusion between the fall in price of a particular article and a general fall in prices. A general fall in prices means not that things have become cheaper but that the value of money, the length of the yardstick, has been altered, and this is just what ought not to happen. If some new invention were suddenly to reduce by 52 per cent. the amount of human effort required to produce every one of the commodities which enter into the Board of Trade Index Number of Wholesale Prices, there is no equitable reason why the money price of each of these commodities should go down by 25 per cent. If this were to be the result, the first effect of the new invention would be to give an uncovenanted benefit to all creditors and to increase in terms of commodities the burden of all money debts. This would mean, as all big fluctuations in the general level of prices always mean, a redistri-

bution of the national income and consequent maladjustment, leading on very soon to the sort of economic and financial crisis we are now experiencing.
On the other hand, if prices remained unchanged,
the advantages of the invention would go to the
entrepreneur in the form of increased profits and
opportunities for expansion, and to the wage-earner
and salary-earner in the form of higher wages and
salaries and increased employment, leading to an
all-round increase in the standard of living, while
the creditor's income would bring him just as much
as before, so that he would be in no way damaged.

If I put stable money in the forefront of what is
needed for successful national reconstruction, it is
because national planning ahead is so difficult as to
be almost impossible without reasonable stability of
prices. It is equally true that success in securing
stable money is hardly to be hoped for without much
greater conscious direction and forward planning in
other parts of our economic and social and political
life. In the financial sphere careful attention will be
required to the subject of saving and investment.
In past years there has been, in fact, much more
direction and control of the flow of capital into
new development, especially external development,
than has been generally recognized, but such direction and control have been unsystematic and hap-
hazard and largely unconscious. We need a new
technique both of saving and of investment.

[98]

And here I should like to say a word on this subject of saving. New capital can be created by saving and only by saving. Some of our troubles in recent years have been caused by a diminution in the rate of our national savings, the result partly of the redistribution of the national income during and after the war. In Russia a gigantic attempt is being made to force savings by keeping down the standard of living to what seems to us an intolerably low minimum in order to provide capital for the Five Years Plan. We do not want anything of that kind here, but we do need all the new capital, that is, new savings, that the nation can provide. Conscious as we have been of the paradox of poverty in a world of plenty, we as a nation have been unwilling to believe—and I think rightly unwilling—that drastic economy and a lowering of our standard of living can be the right way out of our trouble, and unfortunately it has been quite true during the last few years that much of our savings has been of little use to the nation and that further cutting down of expenditure has too often meant simply adding to the army of the unemployed. We must be careful, however, not to draw the conclusion that saving is a mistake. For the individual, reasonable provision against contingencies and against old age is, in a nation of free men and women self-disciplined by an active social conscience, a primary duty to himself and an obligation which he owes to the community. The Planned State will have need of the new capital which his savings create, but the Planned State will use this capital effectively. What has been wrong in recent years is not that there has been too much saving—there has been too little—but that owing to the breakdown of the monetary system and the catastrophic fall in prices the saving has not been effective in creating new capital. The remedy is not to stop saving but to secure stability of prices, after first permitting or bringing about a reasonable recovery of prices, and by means of a new technique of investment to make effective use of the new capital.

Remembering the Altogetherness of Everything I am in some fear that in devoting a large part of this evening to finance I may have left a wrong impression in the minds of my audience as to its relative importance in the comprehensive plan of national reconstruction which is needed for our salvation. Finance is the handmaid of industry and not its master. If it has tended to usurp the place of master this is again largely due to the instability of price levels. With stable money, industry can concentrate anew on its special function of eliminating waste and bringing down the costs of production—not merely the money costs but the real costs, which with stable money will be the same thing.

All along the line we have simultaneously to get to work to overhaul existing methods and practices and to rebuild our institutions. In the economic sphere agriculture, marketing, transport, housing, all need attention in close co-ordination with each other, and all have to be interrelated with the Social Services, with health services, with education, with the problem of provision for our leisured hours. In the sphere of internal politics it has long been evident that tasks are being set for the Cabinet, for Parliament, for the voter, which the machinery of Government, central and local, built up in past ages and during the nineteenth century, does not enable them adequately to perform. They too find themselves frustrated in their efforts just as much as the individual by the complexities of twentieth-century life. It may be that the line of advance will be found in a considerable devolution of powers of self-government to organized industrial councils and new Public Utility Corporations. All this needs intensive study and unprejudiced and clear thinking along new lines. Nor can we stop short with our internal problems. We have to keep in mind always imperial and world contacts, and our planned Great Britain has to fit itself harmoniously into the whole of the twentieth-century world.

The task before this generation is an immense and formidable task. We have first to pull ourselves out of the Slough of Despond into which we have fallen and then to build anew the whole structure of our life in an environment which the marvellous achievements of twentieth-century science are daily making ever more strange and unfamiliar to all but the youngest among us. And we have to do all this without sacrifice of the past, without break of continuity, with full sense of our responsibility for the great inheritance of mankind's spiritual and material achievements in all ages. We may well feel humbly that more is being asked of us than we are able to perform. We may well feel also that our vision of the future is too dazzling for us to be able to bear it.

For the first time in human history the mere problem of daily subsistence has ceased to be the primary preoccupation of a large part of the inhabitants of the earth. There is no reason why in a short time any human being should feel serious anxiety about the provision of food and clothing and houseroom for himself and for those for whom he is responsible. Science offers to us and to the generation immediately ahead of us a standard of living and of material comfort immensely higher than any that has been known to the most fortunate of those which have gone before. Shall we not bend all our energies to the work of making straight the path by which we and they can enter into our inheritance and of fitting ourselves, so far as we can, and without fail helping those who succeed us, to become more worthy in body and in mind and in spirit of the immeasurable opportunities which are offered to humanity of a higher and a nobler life?

V

HENRY CLAY

FROM WHO'S WHO (1932)

CLAY, HENRY, M.A.; M. Com.; Hon. D.Sc. Cape Town; Economist to Securities Management Trust; *b.* 1883; *s.* of James Henry Clay of Bradford and Elizabeth Bulmer; *m.* Gladys, *d.* of Arthur Priestman, J.P.; three *s.* one *d. Educ.:* Bradford Grammar School; University College, Oxford. Warden of Neighbour Guild Settlement, Sheffield, 1907–9; Lecturer for Workers' Educational Tutorial Classes under the Universities of Leeds, London, and Oxford, 1909–17; Ministry of Labour, 1917–19; Fellow of New College, Oxford, 1919–21; Stanley Jevons Professor of Political Economy, Manchester, 1922–27; Professor of Social Economics in the University of Manchester, 1927–30; special Industrial Correspondent of New York Evening Post, 1920–21; Member of Economic and Wage Commission, South Africa, 1925; Member Royal Commission on Unemployment Insurance, 1931. *Publications:* Economics, an Introduction for the General Reader, 1916; The Problem of Industrial Relations, 1920; Post-War Unemployment Problem, 1929.

V

HENRY CLAY

I

THE most surprising thing in the present economic depression is the surprise it excites. Depression is no novel experience in modern industry, and, if it were, it could not be unexpected in the circumstances of 1930–32. For half a generation the Governments of the world have been interfering with the direction and objects of industry and commerce, and interfering on political, non-economic grounds. First by the war, and subsequently by nationalist policies based on considerations of political prestige or social need, they have obstructed old commercial relations and established new ones. Economic considerations have been very largely ignored, and economic arrangements to a corresponding degree upset. The world system of industry and commerce is an intricate and delicate machine, which—like other machines—does not function well when it is upset. I do not criticize this subordination of the commercial object of industry—the pursuit of the largest return at the lowest expense and the endeavour to produce nothing that shall not be worth at least what it cost—; on the contrary; I recognize that industry must always be regulated and subordinated to other more important social aims. But to ignore so extensively this commercial aim, and to substitute such extraneous political objectives as defeating the Central Powers, cementing imperial unity, forcing up the standard of life when trade is declining, increasing taxation to a quarter or a third of the national income, or—to look abroad—expressing by means of trade barriers one's new-won national freedom, boycotting one's political opponents, "larning the Germans to be Germans" by occupying their territory—I need not weary you with further examples—to do this was obviously to impose on the commercial organization of industry a strain it was not designed to meet, and under which it was likely to break down. A century and a half ago Adam Smith explained to us how the business man, if left to himself, was led by an invisible hand to promote an end which was not his own; in the last eighteen years the business man has been led by the too, too visible hand of the politicians to promote an end that turns out to be neither his nor theirs—the collapse of industrial prosperity throughout the world.

My subject is this dislocation of economic arrangements by the war, and the failure to establish a new

equilibrium since the war. Inevitably the previous
lecturers have touched on this subject, but they have
gone beyond it to the consideration of other,
especially monetary, elements in the depression. The
question I shall confine myself to is: "Why and in
what way does a disturbance of existing commercial
relations tend to produce depression and a fall in
prices? I shall refer to the monetary phenomena of
depression only to show that a fall in prices can be
brought about by industrial dislocation quite independently of monetary policy. And I shall apply this
theoretical analysis, such as it is, to the present situation. The crisis, if there is a crisis, is the result of
trade depression operating on the credit institutions
of society; and I shall deal with it only from that
point in view. In considering policy, however, it is
important to distinguish between this element of
"crisis" and the underlying industrial dislocation,
because they call for different measures in their
treatment.

If we reduce our industrial system to its most elementary terms we see that it is a process of exchange. With few exceptions no one produces for
his own use, everyone produces to sell; and selling
and buying are merely the method by which exchange is effected. Most people produce as members
of the personnel of some firm, and firms produce
for other larger firms or for merchants; so that the
business of exchange, of selling and buying, tends

to be concentrated, or canalized. Thus it comes to be controlled by a class that is small in relation to the whole working population, though large in itself, the class of business-men or entrepreneurs. I have reminded you of this very elementary fact of exchange because it is so constantly overlooked. The organization of the modern market is so nearly perfect that we tend to forget that exchange is a two-sided process, and to think of ourselves either as buyers or as sellers, not as exchangers.

Now, exchange being a two-sided process, if buying stops, selling must stop. There is a relation of mutual dependence between sellers and buyers. I mention this equally obvious fact again only because its consequences are commonly overlooked. No seller can go on selling for long, unless he can get a price that covers his expenses; whether he can do so depends on the condition of his customers; and this, on examination, turns out to depend on whether they have been able to sell (at a remunerative price) what they produce. You can, of course, have goods moving one way without exchange—gifts or reparations; but these promote no reciprocal industrial activity. Industrial activity depends on the maintenance of exchange; if exchange stops, industry stops.

One further elementary point. Exchange continues only so long as the parties to the exchange can agree upon terms. Industry continues active only so long as all or the majority of producers succeed in producing what others want, and in producing it at a price at which these others will take it. This is obvious in the case of any particular sale—in the case, for example, of a failure to agree on the terms of sale of labour when there is a strike or lock-out; or in the case of the production of something that misses the fashion and has no sale. What I want you to grasp is that a failure to sell something (with a consequent check to industrial activity) is only one side of an almost inconceivably lengthy and complicated process of exchange, at the other end of which is another failure to sell. Bradford's inability to sell light worsteds at a price that will enable manufacturers to go on employing labour may be the correlative of the Australian farmer's inability to get a remunerative price for the wool out of which the cloth is made, and vice versa; the unremunerative price of British machinery may be both the outcome and the explanation of the unremunerative price of Argentine wheat. Hold up selling at any point because you cannot agree over prices, and you inevitably check selling at other points, because a sale is only one side of an exchange, and if one side stops, the other side must stop.

I have troubled you with this tedious statement of truisms because the very complexity of the modern industrial process tempts us to overlook them, and because it is only if we bear them in mind that we can understand what happens in a trade depression. To the business man, trade depression presents itself as a falling off in demand, a decline in the quantity of his sales and in the price he can get. This, we have seen, is the correlative of someone else's loss of trade. Our first seller sells less because his customers can buy less; and they can buy less because they themselves are selling less. The terms on which sellers will sell no longer coincide with the terms on which buyers will buy; or, to put it quite generally, producers cannot sell because they will not buy, and they cannot buy because they will not sell. On some terms buying would be resumed, and at some time these terms will be reached and then selling will be resumed.

II

From this point of view the problem of trade depression is an inquiry into the causes of the divergencies between the prices which producers can afford to accept and the prices which consumers of their products can afford to pay. Such an inquiry could be pursued along two lines. Either we can study the divergence of cost and selling prices; if we do that, we shall be led very largely into the field of monetary policy and of price movements in general. Or we can follow the line of studying the mistakes in the direction of production, the misdirection of production, which has resulted in labour and capital being specialized to purposes for which no one is prepared to pay, or no one is prepared to pay a price that will enable the activity to continue. It is this misdirection of production that I want to deal with, and to point out, among other things, that by itself, without any alteration in monetary policy, it can produce a general fall in prices.

The business man is familiar with over-production as a cause of depression. He meets it in the experience of his own business, and obviously if one industry produces in excess of the amount the market will take at a price that will cover its costs, that industry must suffer a check. If it suffers a check it will contract production, in which case the persons engaged in it will have their incomes reduced; earnings and profits will both come down, and they will be able to spend less on the products of other industries. Thus the depression in any one industry, due to misdirection or over-production of its product, will react upon all other industries from which the people in the first industry normally buy; so that a sufficient number of cases of error of this sort, of misdirection of production leading to excessive production of certain commodities, will result, through the loss of purchasing power by the people in these industries, in a spread of depression over the whole field of industry, that is in general depression.

Now it is commonly argued that this cannot happen, because the depression in one industry is compensated for by expansion in others. If one industry produces too much, its prices must come down relatively to other prices. Consumers will have more to spend on other things, and therefore other prices will go up. That argument makes two assumptions which are not always true. It assumes, first of all, that the industry in which over-production has taken place will cut its losses, bring down its prices, and get rid of its excess production, which does not always happen; and it assumes that the people who are saving something on their purchases of this over-produced commodity will spend what they save. The first assumption is not justified, because producers are reluctant to face their mistakes and endeavour by price maintenance schemes and other devices to avoid the inevitable loss; in which case there is no saving to the consumer and yet a check is given to the activity of the industry. The second assumption is not justified, because people's habits of expenditure and consumption are to a certain extent rigid. We make an unexpected saving owing to a fall in price of something we buy: we do not necessarily spend the saving, but for a time leave it to accumulate in the bank. In that case there is no stimulus to other business.

But, you will ask, do not the banks collect these savings and put them at the disposal of other people, so that they are spent and do stimulate other industries? It is true that the banks collect and lend savings; but it does not follow that these savings necessarily stimulate industry. It is not the amount of bank deposits, the amount of nominal purchasing power in the banks, that determines industrial activity, but the rate at which this "money" is turned over. If I decide to save instead of spending, the result is that my bank balance increases; but the bank balance of the firm from which I draw my income diminishes by exactly the same amount, so the total of the deposits in all the banks is unaffected. If, on the other hand, I decide to spend, the result is that my bank balance falls, but the bank balance of the firm from which I buy anything goes up by the same amount; so that again the total of bank balances is not affected.

It is true that if the cash basis is increased, bankers can afford to create fresh deposits by buying investments themselves; but if these deposits remain inactive no stimulus to industry results. Activity of existing deposits can do all that is normally necessary when, as now, dormant deposits are a high proportion of the whole. Saving by consumers takes the form of a subtraction from current accounts and an addition to deposit accounts, or it is left technically on current account, but in fact is not spent, and is therefore the same as if it were on deposit account. This increased proportion of deposit to current account would enable the banks to reduce their cash ratio and increase their ratio of investment; but for the reason just stated this would not necessarily stimulate trade activity. If then we save, and do not use our savings, the result is a slowing down of the rate of industrial activity; that, I think, is what has been happening in the last two years. If it is so, the misdirection of production resulting in over-production in particular industries will not only check these and slow down their activity, but it will react on other industries, which will also slow down; and the savings accumulating in the banks as a result of any falls in prices of over-produced commodities may not be turned over, so as to give support to industry. In that case, there will be a general slowing down of industrial activity.

Any general or extensive misdirection of production will thus tend to bring prices down generally. Directly, it will affect the prices of the commodities that have been produced in excess; indirectly, by reducing the prices that these industries and their personnel can pay for the products of other industries it will tend to bring down other prices. If consumers promptly spend on other things what they save on the over-produced commodities, they will check the fall; but any delay in doing so will give the decline time to spread, and when it becomes at all general they will be inclined to hoard their savings, economizing on their current expenditure and declining to take the risks of investment on a fall-

ing market. The proportion of idle to active deposits
will increase; and presently the volume of deposits
will also diminish as a result of the cancellation and
contraction of advances as trade becomes worse. A
fall in the price level may then be due to the cumulative influence of a number of mistakes in the
direction of industry to demand. Monetary policy
may check or aggravate the decline; but the decline
can be initiated and continued independently of any
change in monetary policy.

Once started, a fall in prices, however caused,
must aggravate trade depression. It produces a divergence between costs, which are difficult to reduce,
and selling prices; and so checks further production.
And by its divergent influence on different kinds of
income it alters the distribution of income and therefore calls for a redirection of production. In other
words, a general fall in prices almost necessarily involves some misdirection of production, because producers cannot immediately divert their activities
from the directions corresponding with the former
distribution of income to the directions corresponding with the new distribution; but the point I wish
to insist on is that a general price-fall may itself be
caused by a misdirection of industry. I insist on it,
because the period of the war and the following
decade appear to me to be a period in which the
misdirection of industry has been the most important influence on industrial activity, and an impor-

tant, if not the only, influence producing the general fall in prices.

It was necessary to make clear the relation between the misdirection of production and prices because price movements have been the most obvious of the phenomena that have accompanied the postwar depression, and no explanation of the depression could be accepted which it was not possible to reconcile with these phenomena.

But it is the misdirection itself that it is my present object to examine. At all times there is some misdirection. This is inevitable in view of the geographical separation of most producers and the customers they serve, and the length of time that production takes from the first initiation of the process of satisfying a want to the final transfer of the finished commodity to the consumer. Consider only the dislocation that must be met and allowed for due to the variations in harvests, to changes in fashion, to the introduction of new methods or new commodities; remembering that every change has its reaction on the customers of the industry which it directly affects. In peace, however, before the war the misdirection was kept within limits, and it was seldom that it involved an unemployment percentage of, say, ten for many months before it was corrected.

III

I turn to the contrast between pre-war industry and the position of industry to-day. Before the war we had mistakes of business men, resulting in over-production at particular times and in particular places. We had also mistakes resulting in under-production, with a corresponding stimulus to the industries concerned. There was a sort of averaging of the risk that industry would not be directed to the purposes on which it could be fully employed; there were a large number of suppliers of most things, and a large number of buyers of most things. The task of keeping supply directed to demand was undertaken by thousands of firms operating independently. It would be unlikely that all those firms would go wrong in the same way. It was more likely that some of them would find the way back to prosperity after any check, and there was no obstacle to their pursuing that way themselves and leading others along it. The result was that taking the twenty years before the war, as far as we can judge, the success of the people who direct industry in keeping industry occupied on the things people wanted and were willing to pay for was so great that on an average there was under 5 per cent. of unemployment, or in other words that over 95 per cent. of the working population could be kept employed. Since 1920, on the other hand, the unemployment figure has averaged over 13 per cent. In other words, we have been able to find employment for less than 90 per cent. of our population.

This does not mean that the directors of industry are any less efficient than they were before the war. What it does mean is that before the war the world's industry was in a state of balance. The different industrial groups in the world were so proportioned to one another that exchange went along smoothly. The war destroyed this balance and the world's industries have never found a new equilibrium. In retrospect, it is obvious enough that war must have this result; but we are so accustomed to rely on the recuperative power of the industrial organization that we find it hard to conceive of a shock from which it might not recover. It is worth while, therefore, to remind ourselves of the succession of dislocating shocks to the old balance of industry that the war involved.

The war involved the diversion of resources in men and equipment to war service and munitions production. In the latter part of the war not less than half of the country's economic resources must have been absorbed in meeting war needs. After the war it was necessary to divert them back into channels in which they could meet the normal demands of peace. The task of rediversion was greater than that of organizing them for war, not only because there was no dominating object by reference to which the movement could be controlled, but because the other channels from which they had been drawn were many of them closed by the war. Even in the field of munitions supply the post-war openings were reduced; before the war an eighth of the capacity of the British shipbuilding industry was absorbed in the building of warships, to-day the industry with an expanded capacity gets no business at all from this source.

If the war expanded some industries it contracted others, both because their labour was required for the army and munitions and because their markets were closed. The splitting of the world into two hostile camps involved an immense diversion of international trade. The blockade and restrictions on shipping involved an almost equally important diversion. The United States expanded its wheat acreage to fill the place left vacant by the loss of Russia's exports; the mills of Japan and India were expanded to supply the markets that Lancashire could not supply. But this diversion of trade involved a duplication of capacity; for the war did not permanently contract Russia's capacity to supply the world with wheat, or Lancashire's capacity to supply it with cotton manufactures. The simultaneous expansion of the munitions industries throughout the world created a vast problem of excess capacity for these industries, once the demand for munitions came to an end; the duplication of supplies of many of the most important agricultural staples and commoner manufacturers created a similar problem of excess capacity for their producers, once the obstructions to trade that the war created were removed.

The nationalist economic policies of post-war Governments after the war continued the good work of the war. Australia decided to build up her own woollen industry by putting a prohibitive duty on imported manufactures, and just as the depressed Yorkshire industry was recovering, her next best market, Canada, decided to do the same. Now England follows suit, and French spinners are looking for mills in England in which to duplicate the already excessive capacity for woollen spinning and weaving from which the industry in every country is suffering. The story of cotton is the same. In every country the industry has been depressed, even when other industries were active, because in the world as a whole there is more machinery than the total demand will employ. The coal industry's troubles are rooted in the same policy. When the Silesian boundary was under discussion the delegates of Poland and Germany both insisted that the coalfield was essential to their national life; a few years later negotiations over a commercial treaty between the two countries were held up, not for months but for years, because the Germans refused to admit any

Polish coal, and the Poles insisted that they must
be allowed to export to Germany this essential of
their own national life. In shipbuilding the leaders
of the British industry have sought to deal with the
difficulty by taking upon themselves the burden of
reducing excess capacity; they have induced their
fellow-shipbuilders to bind themselves to pay a levy
on all new contracts, on the security of which they
have raised a loan to buy up and scrap redundant
shipyards.

Now excess capacity on the scale of these post-
war examples was rare before the war. It is a cause
of depression in large industrial areas, and involves
to some extent all the industries that are dependent
on these areas for markets. The petrol-distributing
companies find that their sales per head of population in the industrial towns of the North-West and
North-East are only half what they are in an industrial town of the South Midlands or South-East;
the oil industry (which is suffering from excess
capacity due to other causes) will be assisted to recovery if and when Lancashire and Tyneside have
found some new outlet for their energies, to replace
their lost trade in cotton goods, ships and coal.

The financial strain of the war left a long train
of industrial and commercial dislocation, which still
hampers trade recovery. In every country to a
greater or less extent the expense of the war was
met by inflation, which forced up the price level.

As we have seen, any change in the price level brings about a redistribution of the national income and calls for some redirection of the country's industry. Both in countries in which the rise continued until the currency collapsed and in those in which it was checked and followed by a fall, an abnormal strain was put upon the price structure. The price structure expresses the relations of the different groups of producers in the community and any disturbance of it disturbs the regular process of exchange between them.

Two elements of dislocation date from the war which are of exceptional influence in explaining the world depression of the last two years—the uneconomical movement of exported capital, and the destruction of the balance in the world between agriculture and industry. For a dozen years the world has been in a condition of unstable equilibrium, but these two factors can be distinguished as contributing most clearly to the recent world-wide collapse.

Before the war one could, I think, say of the export of capital that it was twice blessed. It was an export of capital that was surplus to the needs of the country making it, to countries which had resources to be developed and which could, out of the development of those resources, well afford to meet the service of their loans and ultimately to repay them. Since the war the export of capital has been, on the contrary, twice cursed. In one important case, in the case of reparations payments by Germany, capital has been taken out of a country in which it was urgently needed for local purposes, for the ultimate benefit of France and America, which had a superfluity of capital. On the other hand the voluntary export of capital, particularly from America, in recent years has very largely gone to countries which had, it is true, an immediate need for capital, but were not countries in the condition of Australia or the Argentine, or of the United States in the nineteenth century, where large natural resources were awaiting development if only capital could be obtained. It follows that a large part of the capital loaned, particularly to the countries in Central Europe, and to some extent also the countries of South America and elsewhere since the war, has been lost. It was used for current purposes which did not result in any great increase in the productive capacity of the countries receiving it; yet the recipients are under an obligation to pay interest on it, and ultimately to repay the principal. This they cannot do; there is the same difference between pre-war and post-war export of capital that there is between forcing water uphill and letting it flow naturally downhill.

The other factor is the loss of the balance between agriculture and industry. This can be traced in the movement of agricultural and industrial prices. Ever since the war, although both until last year have been above the pre-war level, agricultural prices have always by that standard been lower than industrial prices. There has been, ever since 1920, a tendency to over-production of the chief agricultural staples. America, we have seen, expanded her wheat production during the war to take the place of Russia. After the war Russia came back, but America was still there. In commodity after commodity we find excessive capacity, over-production and agricultural losses.

While the war was primarily responsible for the disturbance, the agricultural countries have themselves in large measure to blame for its persistence. In the first place, they have endeavoured, by various price maintenance and control schemes, to prevent agricultural prices from falling to a point at which stocks would be cleared and further production checked. Rubber, wheat, sugar, coffee, cotton, wool—all have been subject to experiments of this sort since the war, in every case with the same effect; in every case the control has been incomplete, but has kept prices up for a time at the cost of a large accumulation of stocks, at the same time stimulating further production outside the area of control, which has ultimately led to such an accumulation of stocks that prices have collapsed more precipitously than they would have done if no control had been effected. The same situation has occurred in

the case of certain metals, particularly of copper and
tin.

In another way these countries have aggravated
their own troubles, by their protectionist policy. If
you draw up a list, as was done at the International
Economic Conference at Geneva in 1927, of countries in the order of the degree in which they have
raised their tariffs since before the war, you will
find that nearly all those at the top of the list are
countries like the Argentine and Australia, which
depend mainly on the export of agricultural produce, and the export of agricultural produce to
European industrialized nations. By excluding imports from those industrialized nations, they caused
unemployment in those industrialized countries.
They still have to send their agricultural exports to
these countries, and they have to take what these
countries can pay. Prices are low because they have
forced down prices. They put European industrial
workers out of work and on to the dole, and they
have to accept for their agricultural exports the
price which a man on the dole can afford to pay. I
think nothing illustrates better the failure of Governments all over the world to see the truth of the
economic situation than the attempts that they have
made since the war, by protection and subsidies and
cheap credit and price maintenance schemes and
assisted emigration, to put men on the land, when

the great need of agriculture was to get men off the land.

These are only a few instances of the kind of dislocation that industry and commerce have suffered since the war. Even had there not been these shocks, the war would still have upset the world's equilibrium for another reason. All the time there is bound to be some shift of industry as old industries decline and new ones grow up. Perhaps the shift might involve a change amounting to 5 per cent. of the occupied population in the year. To such a change industry can adjust itself quite easily; but if, owing to war and the inflation that attends a war and that attended the post-war boom, there is for eight or ten years a check to this normal small adjustment year by year to changing conditions, then your annual 5 per cent. adjustment accumulates to a revolutionary change. To some such shift certain industries were peculiarly exposed. All the years from 1914 onwards, the coal industry was having its position in world markets undermined, not only by the opening of new coalfields, but by the development of fuel-economizing devices, such as the greater use of electricity, and by an alternative source of power in oil. Yet the industry in the world as a whole enjoyed prosperity until 1924. Then, after the French evacuation of the Ruhr, the German coal industry came into production in full blast and the unfortunate industry had to face ten years' accumulation of little changes, which it might have met with ease from year to year, had adjustments been made when the changes happened, but which had a devastating effect when the accumulated changes of ten years had to be met all at once.

The resulting situation is that in all the older industries, in which technique is standardized, there is excess capacity. When a new country sets out to develop industries by protection and subsidies, it selects these older industries because they are the best understood. Similarly in all the staple agricultural crops you have excessive stocks. The world has allowed its activities to be contracted into too narrow a range of occupations, and exchange has slowed down as a result. This process is well illustrated by a remark which an American friend of mine made. He often met Americans three or four years ago, who expressed concern at the condition of this country; his reply was that, if in America, or indeed any other country, you took cotton and wool and linen, bituminous coal and shipbuilding—the older industries in which we have specialized—and put them together in one State, you would have an area of depression greater than anything in England, because those industries are depressed throughout the world. They were as depressed in the United States as they were in this country; but this country, being the pioneer of them, had a larger proportion of her activities invested in them. As I have said, the root cause of this excess development is that these old industries are standardized and can easily be transplanted; in the words of a friend of mine, who has the misfortune to own a cotton mill, "You can pack a cotton mill in a basket in Oldham and unpack it in Mozambique, and the creature will begin to purr as soon as you put it on its new mat."

The "crisis" is the cumulative result of this depression. More and more people have become insolvent as a result of the world-wide misdirection of production with its reactions. Debts have become a heavier and heavier burden as prices have fallen, until in certain countries (not in this) the solvency of banks is doubted; and in many countries, which have only recently been able to put their currency systems on a stable basis after the war, the fear is now rife that they will be unable to maintain a stable currency.

IV

How did depression disappear before the war? There were usually three forces making for the correction of mistakes of the type I have described, making for the redirection and recovery of industry. The first was that stocks were consumed and people had to start buying again. One can make last year's suit last next year and the year after, but at some point one has to make up one's mind to incur the

expense of a new suit. In the second place, costs
were reduced, so that it became possible to stimulate
renewed buying without the producer being involved
in further loss. In the third place, the flank of depression would be turned by the development of
new processes in industry, the discovery of new
markets, the creation of new industries—in one way
or another by industry finding new outlets in which
it was possible to give full employment and still
cover costs on the price received. Since the war there
has been a much greater degree of dislocation than
anything of which we had experience in the fifty
years before the war. But, apart from this, there
has been also a lower degree of adaptability and
elasticity in industry than pre-war industry showed
when the need for adaptability was far less.

Instead of stocks being absorbed, you have had
them maintained by such devices as the Federal
Farm Board scheme or those of the Brazilian Coffee
Institute and the Canadian Wheat Cooperatives. In
the industrial field, instead of excess capacity being
eliminated by the bankruptcy of the weaker producers, with the result that industry fell into the
hands of a smaller number of more efficient con-
cerns, you have had large numbers of redundant
firms—that is, redundant to any probable demand for
the products of the industry—kept in existence by
creditors, particularly by the banks, who always
hope that trade will recover and that they will be

able, by carrying their debtors a little longer, to secure repayment of the loans they have already made.
This practice has an effect on reduction of costs, because it prevents the concentration of industry in
the most efficient hands. The reduction of costs has
also been prevented by the rigidity of English wage-
rates. The maintenance of wage-rates in a period of
falling prices may be desirable on other grounds;
but if one wishes to sell to agricultural countries,
and agricultural prices are tending steadily downwards, as they were even before the recent catastrophic fall, one must be prepared to cut prices to
them, and that has been impossible. This rigidity is
an unintended result of the unemployment insurance
system. The people who make wage-rates are trade
unions. Before 1911 the trade unions provided the
only unemployment benefit; therefore they were
careful not to put wage-rates too high, or to insist
upon conditions that made inevitable a contraction
of employment; now that they have not to keep
their own unemployed they tend to resist any alteration in rates or modification in conditions. The
Trade Mission to the Argentine two or three years
ago brought back a case of a trade in coloured
cotton goods which we have lost to the Italians. We
had lost it by a difference in price which was exactly
represented by the additional payment made to a
Lancashire weaver on an old piece-rate price list for
any work in which he used coloured threads; the

work involved is unaffected, but it has hitherto been impossible to eliminate anomalies of this kind.

Finally, we have checked the forces making for redirection, for turning the flank of a depression, by heavy taxation of the profits which would otherwise have financed the extension of markets or the discovery of new markets, the re-equipment of industry or the opening of new industries. Before the war British industry did not come to the London capital market for its capital. The London market operated mainly for the export of capital. British industry expanded out of the profits made in British industry. If these are subjected to a 5s. income-tax, and no exemption is made in favour of profits which are retained to finance the business, expansion must be handicapped. The earning of profit is the best evidence that a business can expand; taxation at the rate of 5s. in the £ in income-tax with sur-tax added must inevitably in the case of all the small firms slow down the process of adaptation and redirection and expansion in new directions, which is so urgently needed, and in which these small personal businesses usually lead the way. The objects on which the taxes are expended may be eminently desirable, but there is no reason why the necessary taxation should not be raised elsewhere, in order to relieve taxation at this point, where it has an obviously depressing effect upon industrial expansion.

A couple of years ago Mr. Loveday, Secretary of the

Economic Section of the League of Nations, pointed out that this country was losing ground when compared with other countries by the standard of export trade. Whether compared with countries that had pursued an inflationist monetary policy or a deflationist monetary policy, with countries which pursued a policy of high Protection or a policy approximating to Free Trade, this country made the worst showing. I suggest that the explanation may be found in the fact that in this country we have done most to prevent the necessary adjustments called for by the dislocation caused by the war; and that the underlying causes of this failure are that we have the strongest banks, the most generous system of unemployment insurance and the highest burden of direct taxation.

V

The title of these lectures invites contributors to indicate the way of escape. This implies an optimism which I find it hard to feel. In looking to the future I suggest it is important to distinguish between the immediate crisis, which is the threat to the credit institutions of the world, and the underlying problem, which is the misdirection of the world's industry, the loss of equilibrium between different groups of producers, which can only be corrected by some redirection. The immediate problem, the problem of postponing and preventing a collapse of the credit

institutions and currencies of Europe and other
countries, presents itself in a different form in
different countries. In America they are endeavouring to anticipate a further drain of gold by widen-
ing the basis for the creation of credit and currency.
On the Continent and in most agricultural countries,
or those most dependent upon agricultural exports,
I see little hope of preventing a collapse unless there
is a drastic writing down of debts. It must begin
with the political debts, reparations and interallied
debts, because these have least economic justification; but it cannot stop there, and I do not see any
possibility of ever recovering payment of *all* the
loans that have been made to Central Europe, to
South America, even to some of the British Dominions. In these circumstances the creditors and the
creditor countries improve their security by some
writing down of their claims; they had much better
keep their debtors alive than put them in a position
in which they can pay nothing at all.

In our own country the problem calls for less
drastic measures. We are, I think, better off than
any other country in the world compared with a
couple of years ago. In no countries do figures of
consumption of staple foods and elementary luxuries show less falling off than in this country; indeed,
the only industries which seem able to resist the depression are things like tobacco, chocolates, cinemas
and wireless, which are not luxuries of the rich ex-

clusively. The chief danger to this country is a continuance of the slowing down of industrial activity (and of the fall in prices which must inevitably accompany it) of which there have been renewed signs after the slight recovery of the last three months of last year. May I remind you again of the very brief and inadequate analysis I attempted of the relationship between spending and industrial activity. If you spend you keep industry going. You can spend on the satisfaction of your current wants, or you can spend on durable goods, buildings and machines, on adding to stocks and so on—in other words, on capital goods, in which case we call spending "investment." So long as you spend or invest you keep industry going, but if you stop spending on current goods and do not invest your savings, or hand them over to someone else who does, you tend to stop industry, and industrial activity declines. There is no particular merit or virtue, if you can afford to spend, in saving, unless you save in order to invest.

In the position the country is in to-day the only authority or person that can start a spending movement big enough to restore appreciably industrial activity is the Government. Such expenditure is criticized on the grounds that the Government should practise the most rigid economy. This criticism seems to me to turn on a misconception of the nature of economy. It is obviously economy to meet your current expenditure on current objects out of your current income; it would be unsound for the British Government to go on meeting the cost of unemployment relief, for example, by borrowing, because that is a current need exhausted in the course of the current financial year. But if the object of expenditure is some capital purpose, an improvement in communications or amenities or a housing scheme, an object which will last many years, and will give its return over many years, then it is not uneconomical, it is merely ordinary financial common sense, to finance the expenditure by a loan. Arrangements should be made to ensure that the loan is repaid by means of a sinking fund within the life of the object on which the expenditure is incurred; but to object to borrowing for such a purpose is merely to ignore the distinction between capital and income account. After all, the income-tax authorities do not allow us to charge as expenditure, to be deducted from income for tax purposes, any capital expenditure; why should the Government itself ignore the distinction? If a private individual needs a house and he borrows from a building society a sum of money which he will repay over the next fifteen or twenty years, he is commended for his thrift. Why should any different principle be applied to a housing scheme initiated by a Government or other housing authority?

There are objects enough, *within the present*

sphere of Governmental activities, on which capital expenditure is possible and desirable. Mr. Dennis Robertson has invented the slogan "Rebuild South London"; undoubtedly the unprejudiced visitor from the provinces sees many things in London that seem better worth pulling down and rebuilding than Waterloo Bridge. I need not detain you with instances. It is true that between 1923 and 1929 we did spend heavily on capital objects of this sort. Probably we delayed trade recovery by so doing. But that was a period of world prosperity. There was little hoarding, little accumulation of idle balances then, and no need to stimulate people to spend them; so that Government intervention to stimulate spending along particular lines probably diverted capital and labour to these purposes in excessive quantities, and maintained prices at a higher level than was desirable. It is only in the last two years that depression has been cyclical in character, and attributable in any degree to "hoarding," that is to say to idle balances not turning over; and it is only in these circumstances that expenditure on capital objects by a Government can assist. As for the efficacy of such measures, no one doubts that a war would restore trade activity. I sometimes ask people whether we should have solved the unemployment problem if we put all the unemployed into khaki and paid them their present unemployment benefit as wages or pay. The answer is that we should have solved the unemployment problem, but not in the best way. What the world requires is a substitute for war which has not the unfortunate effects of war.

VI

This brings us back to the underlying cause of the depression and the fundamental need, if there is to be any permanent recovery of industry. If the depression was caused by the misdirection of industry, it can be cured only by the redirection of industry into channels along which exchange will be resumed; if the world is suffering from a loss of balance, it can be restored only by the establishment of a new equilibrium.

The measures suggested to meet the temporary crisis fit in with this underlying necessity. We can afford the civic amenities and capital improvements that would start the idle bank balances turning over. If, as Mr. J. E. Barton said recently (*Listener,* February 18th) we are on the threshold of a great age of art, in which all the plastic arts will cooperate with the mistress art in the visible expression of social unity, we can afford to give the movement scope and opportunity. Athens in the age of Pericles, Paris in the thirteenth century, were communities of paupers compared with us. But this expenditure on dignifying our civic life is only a special case of a general tendency to spend more on

THE WORLD'S ECONOMIC CRISIS

luxuries, and therefore to employ a larger proportion of our resources in men and machines in producing luxuries. This tendency is the outcome of
two changes; the success with which the production
of necessaries has been mechanized—everything
that can be standardized on a large enough volume
of output can be produced cheaply to-day, even if
labour is dear; and the decline all over the world in
the birth-rate; with one child less to the labourer's
family than there was in 1914 it is not surprising
that the sales of cigarettes and chocolate have re-
sisted the trade depression.

It is easy, therefore, to see the outlines of a new
distribution of labour that would give a better balance and fuller employment, at least in this country.
More of our industry must be devoted to the needs
of the home market, more to the production of the
commoner luxuries and comforts; less must be engaged in the older manufacturing and mining industries that were absorbing the greater part of the
increase in population before the war. Exports need
not decline in absolute amount, though they may in
proportion to the whole volume of industrial activity; but they must take the form of the finer manufactures and the more difficult to make, in which
our industrial tradition and the adaptability of our
population give an advantage over countries with
labour that is cheaper within its range but also much
more limited in its range. It is easy, I say, to foresee

the outlines of such a redistribution of industry; the difficulty is to know how to get there.

The example of the Russian Five Years Plan has excited the imagination of this generation; it has focused and concentrated a diffused enthusiasm that has hitherto expressed itself in programmes of a New Social Order, Industrial Reconstruction and the like. The practical difficulty that projects of planning have hitherto had to face has been that the people who can do things, and might put a plan through, have no time for planning; while the people who are most fertile of plans are often the last people one would trust with any administrative jobs that mattered. In Russia the union in a small oligarchy of autocratic political authority and a monopoly of economic enterprise has seemed to overcome this difficulty, and has excited the envy of enthusiasts in other countries.

It is at any rate clear that any plan must be drafted with strict reference to the agency that is to carry it out; otherwise plans become mere collective day-dreams, the fairy-tales of a scientific age. Governments are the most important organ of collective action, and are therefore usually contemplated as the chief agent of any plan; in other words, plans tend to grow into party political programmes. Now Governments are not appropriate agents for the execution of long-range plans. "Transient, embarrassed phantoms," their tenure of office is usually too short a period in the lifetime of a nation to remould its economic structure. They tend, as politics become more and more of a full-time occupation, to lose touch with the actualities of industry, and never to acquire the power of judging what is practical in industry and what is not. Their own professional life is exacting; what time can the temporary occupant of the office of Minister of Labour give to the prospects of employment ten years hence, when he has to carry through Parliament a new Amendment Bill to his unemployment insurance scheme on an average twice a year; what consideration can a Prime Minister give to the conflicting proposals of experts concerned with the next decade, when his own immediate political future depends on an international conference that is meeting next month? Governments do not cease to be subject to sectional pressures by taking the description "National," any more than the projects that a Labour Ministry accepts from its middle-class intellectuals can be taken to represent the aspirations of the labourer.

Even if Governments were exempt from the limitations which methods of election and the exigencies of party politics impose upon the individuals who compose them, they would be handicapped in attempting to restore economic prosperity; these defects might be cured—equally they might be aggravated—by substituting a dictatorship for Parliamentary Government. But Governments would still be national—national in their outlook and governed by nationalist interests—while the problem of industry is a world problem. The tendency of national Governments, confronted with a loss of world equilibrium, is to aggravate it by seeking to correct only those effects that are obvious within their own territories. For example, every country is endeavouring to create a favourable balance of payments by excluding other countries' exports; the thing is impossible, because the balances of all the countries of the world must add up to unity (like a bookmaker's book), and the only result will be that in the end no country will be able to get paid for its own exports. The chief tasks with which the Governments of the world have been faced since the war—tasks that no other agency could take off their shoulders—have been the negotiation of the peace treaties and the settlement of the problem of reparations and inter-allied debts; the foresight and harmony with which they have discharged these difficult tasks does not encourage one to burden them with other duties that call for even greater foresight and harmony.

I look for recovery, therefore, rather to the diffused initiative of the more intelligent and enterprising traders, financiers and engineers engaged in industry in this and other countries. I look to them to find openings for the employment of the unemployed, by discovering new wants that are unsatisfied and means of satisfying them at a price the consumer can pay, new processes that will make it possible to stimulate a resumption of trade by price-cuts that involve no loss, and new commercial connections to replace markets that have been lost or spoiled. And the greatest aid that Governments could give to trade recovery would be to remove the impediments and handicaps that hamper the exercise of this initiative.

In this country the most obvious step is to exempt from taxation profits that are not distributed but put back into the business. These are the funds from which industrial expansion in new directions is being financed; to tax them is to slow down and prevent the redirection of industry that is the country's chief economic need. The concession need not cost much—little more than derating; and it might be compensated by taxation of the additional profits that would be earned from the use as capital of these profits. Even if it were a gift or subsidy, it would be one that was applied automatically to the points at which the maximum effect could be secured by the minimum expenditure.

The correlative but more difficult step would be the withdrawal of support from firms that can contribute nothing to trade recovery. In certain industries it is clear that the existing equipment is excessive in relation to any probable demand. Yet re-

dundant firms continue to operate, meeting their
losses out of past accumulations or calls on share-
holders or fresh borrowings from creditors who are
unwilling to cut their loss on past lendings; and, so
long as they operate, they prevent the solvent and
efficient firms from absorbing the whole trade and
recovering lost ground. In the spinning section of
the cotton industry over £25 million has been called
up on shares with an unpaid liability in order to
meet interest charges and trading losses; a third of
that sum applied to re-equipment and the development of new business would have met all the needs
that the most ardent reorganizer has urged. Corresponding with redundant capital is the similar
problem of redundant labour, maintained for year
after year by the unemployment insurance scheme.
The worker's difficulty is greater than the capitalist's, because he has to wait on the enterprise of the
latter to provide new openings; but the Industrial
Transfer Board showed that some relief could be
given merely by moving workers from depressed to
expanding areas; and, so far as transfer is impossible, some improvement in employment would result from a less rigid insistence on piece-rate bases
and other trade conditions devised in the last century when industry was expanding.

If Governments wish to accelerate the return to
some sort of stable equilibrium in the world's industries they will find it necessary to reverse their

post-war practice of protecting and subsidizing industries that cannot face world competition; our own Government will have to use its new tariff as an instrument for breaking down, rather than adding to, trade barriers. Otherwise trade as a whole will diminish, and those industries that are organized for export must decline. It may appear inconsistent to urge this—as it is certainly against the current of policy in most countries—when I have already anticipated that this country must and should come to depend less on export trade. But at the moment we must take things as they are, and at the moment we are highly dependent on export trade. It is not only the proportion of our whole industry engaged in export that is important; but the dependence of particular industries and areas on export, such as on Lancashire cotton, and the integral dependence of all industries on these areas, and of shipping and much of the work of the City on foreign trade. The alternative, therefore, to taking every possible step to restore, or at least assist, these export industries is to see them decline; and, with them, the industries and services dependent on them, to see "grass grow on the streets of Preston," and to face the necessity of pensioning off some hundreds of thousands of workers who cannot be transferred to any other occupation. Is this necessary yet?

I am coming, I fear, dangerously close to a recommendation of *laisser-faire* as a policy for the times; and I am aware, on the highest authority, that *laisser-faire* is dead. If by *laisser-faire* is meant the opposition to legislation that imposes on industry general conditions dictated by the moral sense of the community, I agree that it is dead. I go farther; I deny that it was ever alive, for such legislation has always existed, and such regulation has been advocated by the spokesmen of *laisser-faire* from Adam Smith (whose *Wealth of Nations* is so unlike the popular notions of it) to Dr. Cannan or Brentano. If, on the other hand, it is suggested that we should be better off if the objects of industry and the direction of trade (after complying with the conditions mentioned) were defined by Government for the people who have the running of industry; or, to carry things a little farther, that no one could make, sell or buy anything except by licence or concession from some governmental authority; or, again, to put the same doctrine negatively, that Governments have not enough to do with the functions that already necessarily fall on them—peace, justice and order, sanitation, education, relief, and the regulation of contracts—then I must confess to a clinging to this obsolete doctrine of *laisser-faire.* I feel no *moral* obligation to prefer some tariff commission's choice of the yarn my underclothing shall be made of to my own, and it would awaken in me no sense of sin if my bread contained less than the prescribed quota of British or Dominion wheat. I see little hope of recovery from a widespread extension of the Government's activities in relation to industry when *within its present sphere*—as I indicated it earlier—there is so much more that it might do and so much that it is doing ill.

The existing lines of party division give little opportunity for these views to secure expression, but I suspect they are not uncommon. Really there is only one distinction that matters in politics—the distinction between the people who want to manage other people's lives for them and the people who are content to manage their own. The "managing" type are found in all parties, and in industry as well as in politics. And they are indispensable to society; their force and organizing ability is essential to the efficient working of industry and Government. But, outside Russia, they are divided; they cannot in practice, because each is a full-time job, combine business and the actual administration of government. They can choose their field, but they are restricted to one type of social authority; they can be industrialists or financiers, or they can be Cabinet Ministers or Civil Servants; but they cannot unite in the same person the authority that the organization of industry creates and the authority that the organization of the State involves. And so they balance each other and keep each other in order. That is what *laisser-faire* really involves; so long as these great and good men are divided into two independent camps—the captains of industry in one and the politicians and bureaucrats in the other—the other more humble people who want only to mind their own business and manage their own lives have a chance of living in peace.

VI

SIR W. H. BEVERIDGE

FROM WHO'S WHO (1932)

BEVERIDGE, SIR WILLIAM HENRY, K.C.B., *cr.* 1919; C.B. 1916; Barrister-at-law; Director of London School of Economics and Political Science since 1919; *b.* Rangpur, Bengal, 5 Mar. 1879; *e. s.* of late Henry Beveridge, I.C.S., retired, and Annette (*d.* 1929) *d.* of Wm. Akroyd (through whom held William Ackroyd Founder's Kin Scholarship). *Educ.:* Charterhouse; Balliol College, Oxford (1st Class Math. Mods., 1st Class Classical Mods., 1st Class Lit. Hum., M.A., B.C.L. 1902). Stowell Civil Law Fellow of University College, Oxford, 1902–9; LL.D. Aberdeen, 1923; LL.D. Chicago, 1929; D.Sc. (Econ.) London, 1930; Das grosse Ehrenzeichen mit dem Stern; Sub-warden of Toynbee Hall, 1903–5; Leaderwriter for *Morning Post,* 1906–8; Member of Central (Unemployed) Body for London, 1905–8, and first Chairman of Employment Exchanges Committee; in Board of Trade, 1908–16, as Director of Labour Exchanges, 1909–16, and Assistant-Secretary in charge of Employment Department; Assistant General Secretary to the Ministry of Munitions, 1915–16; in Ministry of Food as Second Secretary, 1916–18; and Permanent Secretary, 1919; Senator of London University since 1919, and Member of University Court since 1929; Vice-Chancellor, 1926–28; Member of Royal Commission on Coal Industry, 1925. *Publications:* Unemployment: A Problem of Industry, 1909 (New Edition, 1930); John and Irene: An Anthology of Thoughts on Woman, 1912; Swish (a submarine war game), 1916; The Public Service in War and in Peace, Peace in Austria, 1920; Insurance for All, 1924; British Food Control, 1929; articles in Contemporary Review, Economic Journal, Statistical Journal, Economica, etc.

VI

SIR W. H. BEVERIDGE

A FEW weeks ago, I read an article by a man who said that he was a firm believer in economists. Whenever an economist told him to do anything, he did what he was told, and he went on doing it until he met another economist, who of course would tell him to do just the opposite. So, at least, the writer of this article declared, and there may be a little truth in his criticism. Economists do differ sometimes. When I first heard of the scheme of these lectures, I was rather alarmed for your mental health. I thought it possible that, if each of us came to you and gave you, as well we might, advice that seemed to differ, you would feel, by the end of the Halley Stewart Lectures, that you understood the world crisis even less than you thought you understood it at the beginning of the course. You might even come to think less highly of economists than you did before you heard them lecture. I hope that this has not happened.

After all, it is not only economists who differ. Doctors differ also. But few people seek advice from separate doctors about the same illness, and if they do, the doctors have a convenient etiquette which saves them from giving advice separately. Doctors do not advise one another's patients, and so do not advertise unnecessarily their differences of view. I sometimes feel that it might be convenient if economists could adopt a similar etiquette; I should like to be able to say to you now, that if there are any among you who feel that they have got the whole truth from any of my predecessors on this platform, they ought not to be listening to me; they should go quietly away, and not risk having their minds thrown into confusion. If, without irreverence to those distinguished authorities and friends of mine, I may carry the medical analogy a little farther, I would like to say that if there are any of you who are by now content to leave yourselves in the hands of Dr. Keynes with his regimen of high feeding, or of Dr. Stamp with his policy of low feeding; if there are any to whom the bedside manner of Dr. Clay has brought confidence; if you think health will certainly be won back by taking Dr. Blackett's Planning Pills or Dr. Salter's International Elixir—then, in the name of Adam Smith, go home. Do not mix your economic medicines. I ought to be allowed to say that, if economists had as convenient an etiquette as doctors.

But I am not allowed to say that, and probably you would not go away at once, even if I did say it.

Possibly you have not found what each of my predecessors has said to you so very different. Of course there have been differences of emphasis, for we arranged that each of us should talk on different aspects of this complicated problem. And there are some proposals on which those who have spoken already have disagreed from one another or on which I am bound to-night to disagree from one or other of them. But, after reading carefully all that they have said here in the past five weeks, I believe that our agreement is altogether greater than our disagreements. Among the previous lecturers Sir Basil Blackett is the one from whom I shall have most occasion to disagree on details; but he is also the one who has expressed most forcibly the truth that seems to me most important, that until we stabilize money or make it neutral to production we shall not avoid crises. Through all our differences some common principles emerge, and by now you should all have fixed in your minds a few main points.

The first point is that this is essentially a money crisis: there is a breakdown in the machinery of exchange and the system of regulating production by prices. The outstanding feature of the crisis is a general fall of prices measured in money.

The second point is that departure of Britain from the Gold Standard, though it is not, I think, a matter for jubilation, has one good consequence that might not have come otherwise. It has cleared the ground of one difficulty in the way of thinking out the money system of the world afresh. The Gold Standard system built up in the nineteenth century is no longer in existence over the greater part of the world. We can decide to try to put it back and work it better, or we can decide to try something else.

Third point is that this crisis is a world crisis, a common disaster of all the world. As such, it is a disaster that is only going to be made worse if each nation thinks purely nationally, thinks or acts in a narrow, selfish spirit. Though it would not be true to say that the crisis has been caused by nationalism, it is to excessive nationalism in the shape of war debts and reparations, of tariffs, of financial policy, that the crisis owes much of its exceptional severity.

From what I have read of their lecturers I believe that all my predecessors would subscribe to those three points, as I do. Let me take the last of the three as my own starting-point to-day. The subject of these lectures is "The World's Economic Crisis and the Way of Escape." I want to emphasize the second word in that title. It is a crisis affecting the world that is under discussion. It is from the troubles of a world that escape is to be sought, not only from Britain's share in them or America's share or Germany's.

That there is a world economic crisis to-day needs

no proof. If I may use again words which I have already used elsewhere: "Wherever we look in the world to-day we see distress. We see trade strangled, factories idle, farmers ruined, ships laid up, men by millions rotting in unemployment. That is not because mankind has lost capacity to produce good things, any more than it has lost desire to enjoy good things. Our means for wringing wealth from Nature are unimpaired; the machines are there and the men to work them, but somehow the machines are not being worked." [1] The fault lies not in the technique of production but in the economics of production or exchange. The world's crisis is economic.

In this common misfortune of all or nearly all the world, each country has its special fate and problems peculiar to itself. For years before this crisis, while many other countries prospered, we in Britain had our million unemployed; we lost steadily our former share of the world's trade. It is easy to see why we had those special troubles. First, we are the oldest industrial country, and have become fixed in old ways. During the nineteenth century, working our coal and iron before others did, we got rich easily, and we thought that this ease would last for ever. An occasional economist, like Jevons, might tell us the truth and warn us to look ahead; but

[1] Wireless talk to America, January 10, 1932. (Printed in *New York Times*, of January 11th.)

those warnings fell largely on deaf ears. As a people we did not realize that we were richer than other peoples, not because we were cleverer or better furnished with natural resources, but through the accident of having started first. That accident helped us then, but now it is a disadvantage. Others have learned by our experience, have worked virgin resources as rich as ours, have not been tied down by bad habits, have put their best brains into business, not, as we do, put an undue share of their best brains into other things than business. Second, we in Britain are the most international of all countries, most completely merged by our nineteenth-century policy in the world's economy, most dependent upon overseas trade, and therefore most hit by the Great War and by those continuations of war which we call war debts, reparations, tariffs. Third, we have not realized how much the world has grown and changed since just before the war, how less dominant a part in it we can play. We have been over-confident of our strength. We have held to rising standards of life and leisure above our European neighbours; we thought we could afford them. We let other people off the war debts more easily than anyone let us off; we thought we could afford it. We put our currency back to gold at par; we thought we were strong enough to do it. We have gone on acting as if London were still the financial centre of the world, instead of being one of several centres all nearly equal. In the last crisis of all, in July 1931, that led us perhaps to try to carry too much of the financial burdens of a world which has grown larger as our relative strength in the world has grown less. Some of those errors were merely stupid; some were generous errors; we need not be ashamed of them all, but they help to account for our special difficulties.

We British, before this crisis, had our national difficulties. In many ways we need to set our house in order. But if there is one thing more certain than another, it is that we should not combat our national difficulties by trying to make things worse for other countries.

Some people have hailed our going off the Gold Standard as a means by which we can damage the trade of other people and benefit our own. Going off the Gold Standard has helped us in certain ways, but it has thrown the trade of the world still more into confusion. The small immediate gain to us on one side has been offset on the other side by loss to the world and to us as in the world. I am not sure that at this moment the gain outweighs the loss. Our going off the Gold Standard is not a ground for jubilation; it marks the failure of ten years' effort to restore the financial order under which the world grew rich before the war. It will be time to throw our caps in the air when we have got back to something as good as we had then or better.

Some people, again, advocate tariffs; most people in this country advocate tariffs at this moment, or with a shrug of the shoulders or a jeer at Cobdenism accept them. I am not going to discuss the tariff issue for this country. But Cobdenism did not stand for international commerce only; it stood also for international good will. Anyone who likes may jeer at Cobdenism—anyone who, after these eighteen bitter years of anti-Cobdenism throughout the world has a taste for more years like them. I am not going to discuss the tariff issue for this country. Of course there are conditions in which theoretically a tariff may help the country that puts it on. But looked at internationally, as a way of escape from a world crisis, can anything be more patently insane than tariffs? Just now, because we have a tariff coming, we are told that foreign manufacturers are planning to build new factories here, and looking for sites to build them. Some of the newspapers tell us that as good news. Well, are these manufacturers opening the new factories here because the factories they hava already are overworked? Of course not. They have factories half idle in Germany or Czecho-slovakia or France. They are going to work those factories still less, or to close them completely and let them go to ruin, while they build new factories here within our tariff. What ghastly folly, looked at internationally! What a remedy for a world crisis!

I know, of course, that Mr. Keynes put that difficulty to himself in his lecture. He asked himself his reasons for supporting or, at least, for not combating nationalist measures like tariffs by Britain and he gave himself the answer: "Britain," said Mr. Keynes, "should be strong, because it is upon Britain's leadership that escape for the world from its troubles depends. We are the people who have the right outlook and so should have strength to take a lead." Well, I am inclined to agree that we are. There are reasons why weakening of Britain's power to-day in the world is bad for the whole world. Because we have wandered all over the world, because we have invested our money all over the world, it is easier for us to think internationally than for most other peoples. One of the secret springs of economic and political disorder to-day is that there has been a great transference of international power from us, who have been internationally minded, to other great countries which are not yet so minded, to America which is too young and isolated, to France which is too old and too fond of remembering the past.

But if the justification for strengthening ourselves is that we are better internationalists, to strengthen ourselves, even if we could do so, by aping the foolish nationalism of others destroys that justification. To try to better ourselves in that way invokes reprisals. To try to better ourselves in that way is suicide. We depend upon the world's prosperity more than any other nation. We should seek to strengthen ourselves at home, so that we may be influential abroad, but not by means aimed directly at the trade of others.

Let me come back from our national troubles to the world's economic crisis. Let me explain, in doing so, that I propose to speak, not as Professor Clay did, of the whole period since the war, but of what has happened in the last three years. The crisis means, for me, the difference between the beginning of 1929 and now. What is the essence of that crisis? It is inability to produce steadily. Why cannot the world produce steadily? How is the productive machine of the world driven along and guided? It is driven along by the motive of profit, it is guided by prices. Its instability depends essentially on fluctuation of prices. We have to ask ourselves, first, why do prices fluctuate as they do? Second, what makes price fluctuatin lead to such paralysis as we see to-day? Those are two separate questions. Before I attempt to answer them it is necessary, if we are to think clearly about them and reach useful answers, to make certain distinctions.

We have to distinguish three kinds of movement in prices.

There is, first, the movement of prices of particular commodities, relatively to one another. In saying that prices guide production, we imply that the prices of particular articles may vary relatively to one another. It is through those relative changes that guidance is given, that capital and labour are diverted to making something which the consumers want more from making something which they want less. Variation of individual prices is essential to the capitalistic system.

There may be, second, a general movement of prices initiated from the side of production. If, by an improvement in the efficiency of industry, the production of goods of any kind is increased, without any change on the side of money, the price of those goods will tend to fall; if improvements affect a number of important commodities at once, there may easily be a fall in the general level of prices. If no change is taking place on the side of money, a rapid development of industrial technique, such as has been seen in America and Germany since the war, would be accompanied by a fall of average prices.

There may be, third, a general movement of prices initiated from the side of money. What we have in this crisis is a change of this third kind, a fall of prices representing deflation of money. That is what we are concerned with in the first instance. But, as you will see later, it is essential to bear in mind the other kinds of price movement which I have named—the relative changes of individual prices, and the general changes initiated from the side of production.

For the moment let us look at this deflationary fall of prices initiated from the side of money. Since the last quarter of 1929 wholesale prices have fallen throughout the world by something like 30 per cent.; the general level of these prices is not much more than two-thirds of what it was two and a half years ago. The fall is not equal for all kinds of goods, but it is general; it is not a fall in cereals alone, or agricultural products, or minerals, or any other single article or range of articles. It cannot be explained by disproportionate production of particular things. Equally it cannot be explained by over-production of all good things. The world, having managed its production admirably up to the middle of 1929, did not then suddenly begin producing too much of everything and set prices falling; on the contrary, it began to produce less and has gone on producing less and less, but has found buyers with proportionately even less money with which to buy. The fall of prices with which we are concerned is initiated from the side of money. It is a deflationary fall of unexampled violence.

That is the outstanding feature of the crisis. Three further propositions can be laid down about it.

First, the deflation is a deflation of credit rather than of gold. There is less purchasing power in action in the world to-day than there was two years ago, but there is not less gold. There is actually more gold in the central banks of the world now than there was in the middle of 1929, and though the distribution of gold has altered somewhat, it has not altered in any catastrophic way, in any way at all corresponding to the difference between the prosperity of 1929 and this depression of 1932. It is the control of the credit superstructure on gold that has gone most wrong to-day. What makes possible the large swings of prices through inflation upwards, through deflation downwards, is the fact that most of our money to-day is not gold but credit, a kind of purchasing power that can be created by bankers and business men between them, by merchants selling on the instalment system and in many other ways.

It is this elasticity of credit that makes these great price movements possible. What makes them not merely possible, but actually come about? I cannot to-day give an answer to that question on which all economists would agree. The causes of credit fluctuation are still a matter of dispute between those best qualified to judge, but I submit as my second proposition, not actually agreed by all economists, but likely to be agreed in future, that the causes of each deflation of credit are to be found in some preceding inflation, and that the cure of the trade cycle must be sought in preventing the upward movement of prices rather than in trying to stop a downward movement, once it has come. Inflation and deflation cannot be divided; the first inevitably brings on the second.

My third proposition is that the degree of dislocation that can be caused by a deflationary fall of prices depends upon the extent to which it encounters rigidities in the economic system.

An absolutely general change of prices, that is to say one that applied equally to all transactions of all men, would make no difference to anybody. As was said by David Hume long ago, it would only mean altering the counters in which men reckon. But an actual fall of prices never does apply equally to all transactions of all men. An actual fall of prices through deflation has two disturbing effects. First it discourages production through the time element that enters into production. It discourages production because, if prices are falling through deflation, those who under our economic system control production become afraid to buy raw materials and pay for labour to produce things; they fear that, when they have produced and seek to sell, prices will have fallen further, and destroyed their expected profit. Second, a fall of prices has the disturbing effect of altering the real value of all obligations fixed in terms of money. It makes all debts more burdensome to the debtor, more advantageous to the creditor. What we are accustomed to describe as a general fall of prices causes dislocation just because it is never absolutely general, because it affects some transactions and not others, because it encounters rigidities of various kinds.

The fall of prices which has overtaken the world in the last three years is more violent than any known before and has met with unexampled rigidities in our economic structure. There are for some countries, not all, the rigidities of internal debts; for some, not all, countries because some have practically cancelled their internal war debts by inflation and depreciation. There are for most countries the external debts, some arising before the war, some arising out of the war as reparations and war debts. There is an increased rigidity of debenture interest. There is a new rigidity of wages, fostered in some countries by an unwise insurance system. In the special circumstances of the post-war world, any deflationary fall of prices would be more disturbing than a fall in times before the war, when the economic system was more fluctuating, when there were fewer rigidities of debts, wages, debenture interest, and the like.

Let me sum up in a few sentences the essentials of the crisis. It has come about through a fall of prices initiated from the side of money, a deflationary fall of prices. That fall has produced unexampled paralysis—it has probably itself been made greater—because it has met with unexampled rigidities of the economic system. Though the deflation of purchasing power and consequent fall of prices may be described as the cause of the crisis, the deflation itself is probably an inevitable sequel of a previous inflation. Inflation and deflation cannot be divided. They are inflation and deflation of credit rather than of gold. That is the crisis, as shortly as I can put it.

The crisis of to-day represents a failure to manage credit, to avoid alternate inflation and deflation of purchasing power. There is a flaw in our machinery for making and unmaking purchasing power: it is not under control. If you look back into history you will see that, from the earliest times, the making of money, of purchasing power, has been a thing which men have thought should be controlled by one authority in the State, should not be entrusted to many authorities or to private caprice. That, I believe, is a bit of basic common sense in economics. The making of purchasing power is a privilege too important to be allowed to a subject. The reasons for State control in early times were that it was essential for people to know what was good money and what was not. All money must bear the King's stamp. The making of money, moreover, gives the chance to the maker of enriching himself at the cost of his fellows; to make fresh money, to put fresh purchasing power into action, tends to raise prices; but prices do not rise at once, and the man who gets the extra purchasing power

SIR W. H. BEVERIDGE

before prices rise can command a larger share of all
the good things that the community is making. For
this and other reasons, making money has been the
King's privilege ever since there were kings. Such
indeed is the possible advantage of money making
that most peoples have thought the unrestricted
power of doing so too dangerous even for the King
or the Central Government. The King might misuse
his power; in Tudor times in England he did misuse
his power to depreciate the currency; in the late war
and after it many Governments followed this
example, and took to the printing-press. Insistence
that all money should be made of some material
such as gold, whose stock cannot be added to
rapidly, which does not disappear in a night, is like
introducing a constitution to regulate the power of
the King. It is a limitation on the power of making
money.

But gold is not our money to-day. Nearly all our
transactions are done by credit, and credit is made
and unmade daily by thousands of private citizens,
by bankers for business men and by sellers for customers. Such machinery as we have for controlling
that—through the operation of central banks—is
not sufficient for its purpose. The making and unmaking of purchasing power has fallen into an
anarchy, and from the anarchy spring the alternate
inflation and deflation which make our booms and

depressions. Unless we can restore effective control and stabilize purchasing power we shall never escape from crises.

That was the main theme of Sir Basil Blackett's lecture; he put stable money in the forefront of what is needed for national reconstruction. But while I agree with that aim, while many who in other ways are farther from Sir Basil Blackett's views than I am will agree with that aim, I cannot help feeling that he underestimates the practical difficulties of getting there. I wish that I thought with Sir Basil Blackett, that "stable money was within our grasp to-day."

Let me put the difficulties as I see them. First, it is easy to say that the function of the central banks of each country ought to be to make purchasing power stable; it is not at all easy to say how they can or should act to bring this about. Instability of money arises from the fact that so many separate banks can and do lend more money than people have saved, can and do create fresh purchasing power. Are we going to take that liberty from them, are we going back to a system in which no bank can lend to A more than B has saved? If not, what powers of control are we going to give to the central bank? At present they are far too limited, and it is hard to see what powers would be sufficient. I certainly am not in a position to-day to say just what should be done, though I agree with Sir Basil

Blackett that something must be done, to change the management of credit.

Second, there is a dangerous ambiguity in the term "stability." It is far from certain that stability of the general price level is a good aim of banking policy; it is certain that apparent stability may be a prelude to a crash. Here is the point of the distinction which I made before—between changes of the general price level initiated from the side of production and changes initiated by purchasing power. If the efficiency of industry is increasing rapidly, the test of monetary health may be, not a stable price level, but a falling one. In the United States of America from 1927 to 1929 wholesale prices remained stable, yet, under the seeming stability and soundness, was opening the abyss into which America and the world have fallen together. Merely keeping the price level stable will not be a sufficient guide to a central bank, however complete its powers. Keeping the wholesale price level nearly stable in America from 1927 to 1929 probably was inflation. Stabilizing money does not mean stabilizing prices.

Third, stabilizing money involves international control, not merely national control. The financial system of the world ought to be one, but can we make it one? It is easy to say, and it is probably true to say, that we shall not get stable money until all the central banks of all countries act as departments of one international bank for the whole world, but when is that likely to come about? Is it a practical scheme, when one considers the close relations between the central bank of each country and the finance of its national Government? It is possible that in the end we may do more for international stability of purchasing power by aiming at doing less.

Suppose, as some have urged, that we should now all over the world just restore the Gold Standard as before, and work it properly as we have not done before. Working it properly means that in each country, by uniform policy, the central banks effectively contract credit or allow it to expand in such a way as to keep the price level of that country in proper relation to the price levels of every other country. If one really got the Gold Standard system working on uniform lines in every country of the world, that would be a unified international monetary system under another name. I am not sure that, in the last resort, the supporters of the Gold Standard and Sir Basil Blackett are as far apart as they think themselves.

To dwell on these difficulties of stabilizing purchasing power does not mean that we should not attempt it; we must attempt it, but we cannot do so with hope of success, unless we see the obstacles that have to be overcome and are daylight-clear

about the aim. We must attempt it; we must, by
international co-operation, seek to suppress the
anarchy of purchasing power which to-day is laying
waste the world. Do you think that an exaggera-
tion? Let me give you three figures. In America the
steel industry is working at a quarter of its capacity,
with three-quarters idle. In Britain there are staple
trades with 40, 50, 60 per cent. of unemployment.
In Germany there are 6¼ million unemployed.
Those are counted figures, not guesses. The nations
must seek to suppress the anarchy of purchasing
power, as they have suppressed piracy and slave
trade, as they ought to suppress war.

But let the aim be clear. It is only the anarchy of
purchasing power that should be suppressed, not
what some people call the anarchy of production.

The world's economic system to-day is capitalistic.
It is a system in which production is guided by the
play of prices. Those who attack the system are fond
of describing it as an anarchy of production. For my
part I think that is a wrong name, and that for two
reasons: First, a thing is not anarchic merely because it is not consciously organized; it may grow
together as a living body does, unconsciously—be
an organism though not organized. Second, there is
a distinction between liberty and anarchy. I am not
sure that there is a philosophic distinction, but there
is a practical one. Liberty is freedom where in the

common interest there should be freedom. Anarchy is freedom where in the common interest there should be control.

Now it is not clear that the freedom of individual business men to produce what, according to their judgment, consumers want and will pay for, will pay for sufficiently to leave a profit after the costs of production have been met—it is not clear that that freedom is a bad freedom, and ought to be controlled by Governments. I am not prepared to say, therefore, that the capitalistic system as a whole is anarchic.

It is here that I approach another point of possible disagreement with Sir Basil Blackett. Frankly, I am a little frightened of what he may mean by planning, or might do if he were given his head there. In so far as planning means that business men undertaking production should look ahead more, or even that they should organize production in larger units more deliberately designed for their purpose, there is nothing to be said against it, there is much to be said for it. But, taken in conjunction with what Sir Basil Blackett said of the breakdown of *laisser-faire,* it is possible the essence of planning may be, in his mind, as it certainly is to certain other people, the limitation of competition. It may be an effort so to regulate production as to stabilize prices for particular commodities—for rubber or tin or wheat or electric lamps or coffee. Of that I am more than doubtful. This is the point of the distinction which I made earlier, between the relative changes of prices by which under a capitalistic system production is guided, and general changes due to deflation of money. Schemes for planning production in particular industries have again and again taken the form of restriction schemes—of avoiding competition, of keeping down the supply in order to keep up the price. Those schemes, as was pointed out in the Macmillan Report, have nearly always, in the end, broken down, and in breaking have added to the difficulties of our time. There is here, I believe, an inescapable fatal danger—the danger of mixing control and freedom. We have to decide either to let production be guided by the free play of prices or to plan it socialistically from beginning to end.

Control and freedom do not mix properly. I learned that, and the country should have learned it, in the war. Let me illustrate it from the special experience of the Ministry of Food. For the first two years of war we had no control of food. We had under Mr. Runciman, now President of the Board of Trade, and then also President of the Board of Trade, a policy of trusting to private enterprise to keep the country fed, assuring those who brought food here that they would be allowed to sell it at a profit; that they would not, when they had bought food and shipped it here, find that, by control of prices, all profit was taken from them. That system worked for two years and broke down only as the war grew more bitter. In the last two years of war it was replaced by another system, by which, under Lord Rhondda, private enterprise for the supply of food vanished completely. Every trader in food became either directly or indirectly a servant of the State, paid not by profits but by salary or by commission for the amount of work he did. That was socialism carried out to the full, complete control as Mr. Runciman's policy was complete freedom. But, between Mr. Runciman and Lord Rhondda, came six months of half control, of fixing prices for some foods and not for others, of fixing prices at one stage of an article and not at others, of fixing prices without controlling supply. That system did not work, and the nation would have starved if it had been allowed to continue. It was an attempt, foredoomed to failure, to mix freedom and control. The people who talk of planning are not usually socialists. They are trying to live in a half-way house between capitalism and socialism. For all the persuasiveness of Sir Basil Blackett, I do not feel certain that his half-way house can stand.

Some of you may say, "We agree with that. We agree that half control would not work, but the free capitalistic system does not work either, and never will work; it is breaking down before our eyes. We have to suppress the anarchy of production and not merely the anarchy of purchasing power. We must try another system altogether, a system of guiding production not by profits but by use, of making money nothing more than a vote by which consumers indicate their judgment of values. We want a system such as they are working out in Russia."

I am not going to condemn the Russian system out of hand as economically unworkable. We tried something like it with food in war-time, and it worked for two years at least. But I do not want to live for ever in war-time, and I am not sure that the system suits any other time, that it can be reconciled with progress or do as well in peace as the present system. One ought to compare capitalism, not with ideal socialism, but with socialism as it shows itself in practice. The Russian experiment, important and interesting as it is, has not yet proved its economic advantages. On the other hand it has suppressed not only the freedom of production, whether you call that liberty or anarchy, but has suppressed also other freedoms which are essential. In the one country that is trying it, socialism still seems to rest on tyranny and terror.

So I, for my part, come back to seeking a way out of the world's crisis within the framework of the capitalistic system, by suppressing, through international co-operation, the anarchy of purchasing power—by suppressing the anarchy of purchasing power and keeping and increasing the liberty of production and exchange. That is the way of escape.

If you ask me to translate those phrases practically, into things that could be done here and now, I encounter difficulties of two kinds—a technical difficulty with the economists, and a political difficulty with the Governments of the world.

The technical difficulty is that though most economists, I believe, would agree as to the need for suppressing the anarchy of purchasing power, as I have phrased it—of stabilizing credit, as others might phrase it—they are not agreed as to just how this difficult operation should be carried out: as to change of banking powers and policy involved, as to the principles on which an international central bank for all the world would control credit, if such a bank were established with full powers. The credit cycle of alternate inflation and deflation is like cancer; we know a great deal about it, but not enough yet to be certain of a cure. There is here a technical problem of economics still unsolved, though not beyond solution, and not, I hope, very far from solution. But if all the economists to-day were agreed upon the remedy for crises, what good would that do? Would the Governments of the world apply the remedy?

Just look at the Governments! Can anyone think them ready for a great and adventurous scheme of international co-operation in finance? Just look at them. I do not say that in any spirit of jeering at Governments or at politicians. The people who form those Governments are not worse than the rest of us—in many ways they are better; at worst they are representative—are like us. In the Governments of the world there are many people of high patriotism and intelligence and experience. But the trouble is that they all have too many things and too national things to do: they all have full-time jobs of carrying on their countries from day to day; they are entangled in a network of party or national manœuvres, of pressing claims to debts and reparations, of conferences and of Cabinet-making, of agreeing to differ. It is so hard for men to-day to rise to power, before they lose the vision to use their power. If we are ever to get a big new thing done in the world, we shall have somehow to disengage for it from daily routine some of the boldest and subtlest spirits of the time. We must find those spirits for our time, strong with maturity, supple with youth; we must find them and trust them and give them power. Perhaps the trouble is that, for our time, those spirits are not to be found; the bodies that housed them once are in Flanders or Picardy or Poland. Perhaps that is why we have no leaders, and such a chaos in the world. Shall we ever stop paying for the war?

The world will not really escape this crisis at all. Even if all economists were completely agreed on a remedy, the Governments would not apply it. The world will not escape this crisis, not if escape means getting out of danger by deliberate thought and action. The world is like a patient with a disease for which the doctors have as yet no cure, except time and trust in his vitality, in the toughness of his system. I believe myself, with Mr. Keynes, that the toughness of the system will pull us through, that the crisis will become less acute of itself, long before we have done anything to better it. If the view that I have suggested above is right, if this deflation is the inevitable aftermath of inflation, the headache after the debauch, then there is not much that anyone can do now to help us; what is wanted ought to have been done five years ago. The most that we can hope for this year—really it is too much to hope for this year—is that the Governments will do something, not to cure the crisis, but to remove some of its aggravations—will deal with reparations and war debts, with some of the obstacles to trade, with one or two needless rigidities. We must plan to avoid another crisis later. We shall not by conscious effort escape this one.

*   *   *   *

The course of lectures which you have evoked, Sir Halley, is drawing to an end. If once again you ask me just what, practically, I should do about the crisis, I answer with another question: "Who do you think you are talking to?" I make that answer not as a schoolboy retort but because I cannot tell you what, practically, I should do until you tell me what powers I am supposed to possess. Actually, as an academic economist not in the counsels of any Government, unconnected with any Government, I cannot do anything at all. I can only try to clear my own mind, and talk when people ask me to talk, and write occasionally, and vote every five years or so at a General Election. If I were Chancellor of the Exchequer, there would be certain things which I could do and which therefore I should try to do. There would be others that I could not do, and therefore should not attempt. I should have different powers and, therefore, should set out to do something different, if I were Sir Josiah Stamp, or the Governor of the Bank of France, or the Prime Minister of England, or the President of the United States. I should direct my thoughts to something different, again, if I were a world dictator. Which of these people am I supposed to be in your supposed question? What I would set out to do depends upon the answer.

I propose to give myself the answer, and assume that I am a world dictator. That is just as easy for me as being the Prime Minister of England, and just as likely for me as being President of the United States. The way of escape from world crises is barred and doubly barred—by disagreement among economists, and by lack of international will among

Governments. Only a world dictator could break his way out now. But I need to be rather more than a mere political dictator. I must be an Aladdin with a magical lamp, with you, perhaps, as a spirit who could work miracles for me, could work the miracle of making all the Governments of the world suddenly and equally sensible. I do not, of course, mean that they need be sensible for all time, but just until we have got things straight again. And I do not mean to go on being a dictator for all time; that would be a dreadful prospect. We have somehow to rebuild a world that will run equably and freely by itself. What miraculous changes ought to be made here and now, to bring back to us an economic system that can be worked smoothly, not by superhuman people, but by ordinary people, not by exceptional Governments, but by the kind of Governments that we are likely to get?

I am going to ask you, Sir Halley, as you sit there presiding over us, kindly to imagine yourself to be a miracle-working spirit, able to do or get done all that I think should be done in the world to make economic life more stable. What tasks should I give you, in what order?

I have no doubt about the first two tasks.

First, you would go and tell all the Governments concerned to drop here and now the whole business of war debts and reparations. Those international obligations arising out of the war are just a continuation of war. They block the way to international co-operation, and are among the worst rigidities of our economic system. They have no moral sanction; they are not like other obligations. Psychologically and economically they are evil.

Second, you would go and tell all the Governments from me that they have to abolish tariffs, not of course suddenly, for that, in high tariff countries, would cause devastation, but under a scheme by which automatically year by year, throughout the world, all tariff walls would slowly sink back into the ground. With them would go all systems of export bounties, sur-taxes and the rest, by which one country tries to get richer at the expense of others. One might need a twenty-year plan to allow time for the industry of each country to readjust itself and put the human race in a position to make the best of Nature's gifts throughout the world.

Those would be your first two tasks. Two days—if I may reckon in biblical days—two days of easy work. For your third day I would send you out to get all the Governments to deal with insurance against unemployment. They have one and all made a mess of that, though they have gone wrong in opposite directions. Some, like America, have done just nothing at all; have not thought of insuring till their house was on fire. Others, like our own, having started on a good scheme, have spoiled it by weakness and sloppiness, have let people get unemployment money without being in any true sense unemployed at all, have made their scheme such that it profited employers and trade unions to make employment more casual, less regular than it need be. All that is foolishness, on one side, as the American attitude is foolishness, and heartlessness on the other side. Each country needs a plan by which everybody has an income of sorts when the industrial system of that country, whatever it may be, cannot keep him busy. But no country should have the kind of plan that promotes and encourages unemployment. From this third task you will see that I contemplate some irregularity of employment, even in a reformed world. I do so because all progress means change, and all change means sometimes dislodging individuals from their chosen occupations; it may mean, in the interests of the community, subjecting them to an interval of idleness till they can find fresh work. No country need have unemployment on the scale that we have had it since the war, but some provision for unemployment is as necessary as provision for sickness or old age.

Those are your first three days of work as miracle-working genie attending on myself as world dictator—abolition of war debts and reparations, scaling down to abolition of tariffs, proper organization of insurance against unemployment. The first two tasks are easy; they need hardly any thought at all. The third task would take a little thinking out, but not much. There is no real difficulty about any of them, given the will to put them through.

But when you came back to the morning of the fourth day, untired and eager, asking to be told your next task, you would find that now at last we had to face a real problem. We have to decide an issue of tremendous difficulty. We have to decide between different ways of organizing the work of the world, and the only two ways we know of do not work properly. I should not be ready on that fourth day to tell you what to do next. I should have to make arrangements for finding out. I should set up a Commission of four or five just and wise persons, well skilled in economics, to advise me. If this were a national affair, I would be tempted to choose my five distinguished predecessors on this platform. But I am just a little afraid of one or two of them; and anyhow the Commission should draw in the best economic brains of all the world, not of one island. To that Commission, however formed, I would give a double task. "First," I should say, "work out for me a plan for stabilizing the production of the world on a capitalistic basis, on the present basis of guiding production by prices." That means, "Work out a plan for abolishing the anarchy of purchasing power, but keeping the liberty of production and exchange. Tell me how it can be done, what change it means in what we do now. Tell me, even if it means abolishing credit creation by banks altogether, going back to cash without credit super-structure at all, or means internationalizing currency completely, making the central bank of every country a subordinate branch of some great international institution."

That is the first half of the Commission's job. The second half is to give me a plan for stabilizing production on a socialistic basis, a plan for guiding production directly by use, and not through the intermediary of prices. "Give me such a plan," I would say, "if you can, even though it means abolishing individual wealth as well as individual poverty. But, as this is essential, you must show me that your second plan can be reconciled with progress and with freedom." The Commissioners, of course, would visit Russia, and you would go with them, to do the miracle of making sure that they got at the truth. In a land on which terror has once lain like a poisonous mist truth does not grow easily.

It would clearly be the end of the fifth day before those Commissioners would come back; they would need two full days for their two tasks. They would have some hard imaginative thinking to do, for they would be making a new financial foundation for our economic life. When they came back I should have to decide between their plans—at least I should have to decide, if they came back with two plans, that each seemed workable. If the Commissioners came back and said, "There is only one of these plans that we are sure will work, smoothly and freely and progressively," of course I would have to choose that one, whichever of the two it was. But if each plan seemed equally workable, or each open to equal doubt, I would choose the capitalistic one for trial. For if the capitalistic plan does not work, at worst we get another crisis like the present, whereas if the socialistic plan does not work we may destroy things of more importance than economic welfare.

One way or the other, by noon of the sixth day I should decide, and in the afternoon you would carry out my decisions. Then, Sir Halley, you and I would both slip gladly out of our dictatorship, out of our miracle-working clothes, to be ourselves again, with no more power to work miracles, with no miracles needing to be done. And the seventh day would bring a world re-made, re-made in economics, but otherwise a world where we could feel at home, a world of work and rest, of personal striving and success and failure, of good luck and bad luck but some chance for all, a world of other human beings like ourselves.